JEREMY BENTHAM

"Swear not at all"

CONTAINING

AN EXPOSURE

OF THE

NEEDLESSNESS AND MISCHIEVOUSNESS

AS WELL AS

ANTICHRISTIANITY

OF THE CEREMONY OF AN

OATH

Elibron Classics
www.elibron.com

Elibron Classics series.

ISBN 1-4021-8670-3 (paperback)
ISBN 1-4021-1720-5 (hardcover)

This Elibron Classics Replica Edition is an unabridged facsimile of the edition published in 1817, London.

"Swear not at all:"

CONTAINING

AN EXPOSURE

OF THE

NEEDLESSNESS AND MISCHIEVOUSNESS,

AS WELL AS

ANTICHRISTIANITY,

OF THE CEREMONY OF AN

OATH:

A VIEW of the PARLIAMENTARY RECOGNITION of its NEEDLESSNESS, implied in the practice of BOTH HOUSES:

And an INDICATION of the UNEXCEPTIONABLE SECURITIES, by which whatsoever practical good purposes the ceremony has been employed to serve would be more effectually provided for.

Together with PROOF of the open and persevering CONTEMPT of MORAL and RELIGIOUS PRINCIPLE, perpetuated by it, and rendered universal, in the two CHURCH-OF-ENGLAND UNIVERSITIES; more especially in the UNIVERSITY OF OXFORD.

Pre-detached from An Introduction to the RATIONALE *of* EVIDENCE.

BY JEREMY BENTHAM, ESQ.

FORMERLY OF QUEEN'S COLLEGE, OXFORD, A.M.

LONDON:

SOLD BY R. HUNTER, ST. PAUL'S CHURCHYARD.

1817.

Printed by Richard and Arthur Taylor, Shoe Lane.

ADVERTISEMENT.

In the state in which it is here seen, this tract was printed A° 1813. In the summer of the year (1813) in passing through the University of Oxford (in which seat of learning above half a century ago the author had taken the last of two degrees), by the hands of a common friend, he caused to be delivered into the hands of one of the Reverend the Heads of Houses, who had been mentioned to him as being of the number of those, in whose instance the hydrophobia of innovation was supposed to be least rabid, a copy of this tract; and staid there long enough to hear of its having undergone his perusal. Of the communication thus made the motive was—a hope, how small so ever, that possibly, by means of the representation thus conveyed, some course might, in that seat of professed piety, be taken, for the abolition of a practice, which, not to profane only, but to reverend and orthodox eyes, had already in more instances than one, presented itself, and had accordingly in print, and in multitudes of editions, been held up to view, as impious.

Whatever other imputations the publication of this tract may be thought to be open to, *precipitation* therefore will at any rate not be of the number: neither on the one part *precipitation*,—nor on the other part, *want of notice*.

After all, this tract might for any further length of time have slept upon the shelf, but for the addition so lately made of the scourge of religious persecution to the yoke of despotism:—for a pretence for punishment as for blasphemy—and that by imprisonment without trial—infliction by every clergyman who is in the commission of the peace—the so recently instituted practice of putting the composition of nobody knows what "*miserable sinners*," who triumphed over piety and sincerity about two centuries and a half ago, upon a level with the discourses of *Jesus*; and, by men by whom the profession of piety has been converted into an instrument of power, the exertions so lately made, to bolster up by the force of their punishments the imbecility of their arguments.

What is here meant is not unknown to Mr. WILBERFORCE. Of the perjury which, so long as he has had eyes to see, has been staring him in the face, let him disprove the impiety, or stand forth at length, and use his endeavours to put an end to it.

CONTENTS.

APPENDIX.

Swear not at all.

Mat. v. 34.

§ 1. *Oath. Incongruity of the assumption, on which its supposed* BENEFICIAL *efficiency is grounded.*

By the term *oath*, taken in its largest sense, is universally understood a ceremony composed of words and gestures, by means of which the Almighty is engaged eventually to inflict on the taker of the oath, or *swearer* as he is called, punishment, in quantity and quality, liquidated, or more commonly unliquidated, in the event of his doing something, which he, the swearer, at the same time and thereby engages not to do, or omitting to do something which he in like manner engages to do*.

Correlative to the term *oath* is the term *perjury*, and its conjugates to *perjure oneself*, *perjured*, *perjurious*; among which *perjury* is understood as designative of the conduct, whether positive or negative, which stands in opposition to the conduct engaged for, as above.

In so far as, in a state of political society, application of this ceremony has been made to the purpose of producing any practical effect, other persons besides the swearer have commonly, in some way or other, borne a part in it: one person at any rate, *viz.* the person by whom the oath is said to have been *administered*: and com-

* In every case, except where the observance promised consists in speaking truth, as in the present case, in which case the oath is said to be *assertory*, (of which immediately) *i. e.* in every case in which the oath is commonly spoken of in the character of a *promissory* one, the term *vow* has moreover been indifferently employed in speaking of it. See, in Cruden's or any other Concordance, the words *Oath* and *Vow*.

monly some other person or persons, by whose authority and order, or at whose instance at least, it has been *administered*, or at any rate *taken*.

The intervention of any such third person is not essentially and inseparably included in the notion of an oath: but it is only in so far as some such intervention has place, that it belongs to the present purpose.

By the ceremony thus described, may be seen at the least two persons, of very different descriptions, over both of whom power is exercised, or supposed or endeavoured to be exercised, viz. 1. Man, the individual swearer, on whom, by means of the eventual punishment in question, the effect of a law, whether prohibitive or compulsive, is produced, or supposed or endeavoured to be produced. 2. The Almighty, who, in the event in question, is supposed or endeavoured to be engaged to inflict such punishment.

Considered in respect of the purpose to which it is applied or applicable, an oath has commonly been distinguished into *assertory* and *promissory*: and, in conformity to this distinction, the *assertory* sort of oath, it will naturally be observed, is the only sort of oath, which belongs to the present purpose;—which bears any immediate relation to the subject of *evidence*,—to the subject of *testimony at least*.

From this distinction a natural inference again is—that, let it even be supposed that, in the promissory oath, condemnation should on any just ground be passed, yet by such condemnation the assertory—the testimonial oath—the oath considered as confined to the purpose of securing trustworthiness to testimony—would, notwithstanding such condemnation, remain untouched.

In opposition however to this notion it must be observed, and upon consideration will be acknowledged, 1. That the nature of the ceremony—the nature of the instrument thus employed—is one and the same, to what purpose soever it be applied: 2. That to every oath alike belongs, in truth and propriety, the quality and name of a *promissory* oath, and that accordingly the *assertory* oath, and thereunder the *testimonial**, are neither more nor less than the *promissory* oath applied to that particular purpose.

By the *promissory*, as opposed to the *assertory* oath, that which a man may undertake for, is—any thing whatsoever that is in his power to do, with the exception of the giving correctness and relative completeness to some *assertion* or other, whatever it be, to which, for the purpose of securing to assertion those qualities, it is applied: by the *assertory* oath, that which is undertaken for is—the giving to some *assertion* those same qualities: but, in both cases alike, something or other is *undertaken for*, *engaged for*, *promised:* in both cases alike an *obligation* is imposed, or supposed, or endeavoured to be imposed: in both alike, for the purpose of giving to such obligation a binding force—a force derived from the religious sanction, —a *ceremony*, and the same ceremony, is employed.

On the supposition that, by man, over the Almighty, *power* should, to this or any other purpose, be exercised or exercisable, an absurdity, than which nothing can be

* In the way in which the testimonial oath is commonly employed and administered, the observation, of its being included, as above, under the promissory, will, it is supposed, be acceded to without difficulty; since, in that case, the ceremony is seen at the first glance to precede the operation which it is employed to influence. By a person from whom assertions or declarations of a testimonial nature are about to be extracted or received, the oath—the ceremony, whereby the qualities in question are supposed to be secured—is performed in the first place, and thereupon comes the testimony by which the promise so made is either kept or broken, and perjury accordingly abstained from or committed.

But, suppose the testimony first given *without* oath: and thereupon, immediately or at any time afterwards, an oath taken, importing that the testimony so already delivered was true?—On consideration, it will be seen that even in this case there exists a *promissory* oath. In the first place comes the ceremony; and with it comes the promise to speak true: thereupon and thereafter comes the assertion to which it immediately applies, viz. that the testimony, which had been delivered antecedently to the ceremony, is true: take away this subsequent assertion, take away the promise to give truth to it, —no assertory oath—in a word no complete oath—at all remains.

Thus much merely for clearness of conception. As to any practical purpose, whether the nature of the case does or does not admit of any assertory oath which is not a promissory one, is a question altogether void of importance.

greater, can not be denied to be involved :—man the legislator and judge, God the sheriff and executioner ;—man the despot, God his slave.

If, in any given instance, on the part of the almighty executioner, any exception to the rule of obedience be supposed, in that instance the effect of the ceremony is nothing ; the case is exactly as if there had been no such ceremony. But if in any one case it be thus inefficient, how comes it to be otherwise in any other case?

Yet this or nothing is what is supposed : this or nothing if the supposition be, that,—after and in consequence of the promise thus made, and the breach of it—the perjury—committed,—punishment—the result of the will and act of God—takes place of course,—that is to a certainty, and in every individual instance.

If, the supposition of absolute certainty being deemed too strong, that of *probability* be substituted to it, still, so long as it amounts to something, and that something produced by the mere ceremony, independently of any other cause,—though it be but a probability, for example, as 1 to 10,—the supposition is in substance one and the same. God is a negligent servant indeed, but still a servant : he disobeys the orders nine times out of ten, but he pays obedience to them on the tenth.

The circumstance by which the supposition of the influence of an oath, over the supernatural agent in question, is saved from the ridicule that attaches upon the supposition of the influence of a magical incantation * over the supernatural agent to which that instrument is applied, is, that in the case of the *oath*, the scene of its influence is

* Magic not being now in fashion, of the existence and exercise of the sort of power indicated by that term, the supposition would be an object of scorn and ridicule. But, of the existence of the ideal power so denominated, the supposition is, in the scale of absurdity, inferior to that of the existence of the power, to the belief of which the ceremony of an oath is indebted for whatever efficiency, whether to a good or a bad purpose, it possesses. By any *magical* incantation, it is only over this or that imaginary being of a subordinate class that the power is supposed to be exercised : by the ceremony of an *oath*, it is always over the supreme being, who thereupon, supreme as he is, is to the extent of this power subject at the same time.

placed in a state of things of which no human being is in this life supposed to be or about to be witness: whereas, in the case of the magical incantation, the scene lies here below, and it is in this life that men are bid to look for it:—the moon brought down upon the earth, as according to the Pagan system: disembodied spirits of this or that denomination brought down or up to the same place, as under the Jewish and Christian, well or ill interpreted.

Quid non carmina possunt?
Carmina de cœlo possunt deducere lunam.

Undertaking to defend the use of this mysterious instrument, what will a man say of it?—That there ever has been or ever will be so much as a single case in which these effects have or will have been produced by it? Will that be his supposition? If so, then is the absurdity thus charged upon it admitted to be involved in it:—That there never has been nor ever will be any such case? If so, then is the supposition admitted to be a mere fiction; and, in proportion as this admission is acceded to, the ceremony is divested of its binding force, and therewith of every useful influence that can ever have been ascribed to it, or expected from it.

The effect, to the production of which, if possible, man and God both are thus sought and supposed to be engaged,—the line of conduct, to the observance of which man is thus sought and supposed to be compelled,—say that it *is*—say that it is *not*—such, for the enforcement of which, punishment, to be inflicted by such hands—punishment, in quantity as well as quality properly adapted to the purpose *ought* to be, may with reason be expected to be, applied:—if *yes*, the punishment sought and supposed to be applied by the oath is *needless*: and, being needless, it is *superfluous*, and on that account improper and mischievous: if *no*, it is *undue*, and on that account again, mischievous: mischievous in a double and more extensive degree: mischievous in a limited extent, by the useless suffering it inflicts on the individual so punished; mischievous to an unlimited extent, in respect of the mischievous line of conduct to which it seeks to engage him, and with a degree of success (of which presently) but too frequently exemplified.

Observe here another absurdity resulting from the supposition attributing a penal effect to this ceremony. Once more—the punishment which, independently of it, is attached to the transgression meant to be prevented—in the present case to mendacity—must in supposition be either adequate or not adequate. If adequate, then is there no need for any additional punishment:—for any such punishment as, in case of mendacity, in which would be included the profanation of the ceremony, would be the effect. If not adequate, then observe the consequence: To his justice, *that* being the attribute here in question, God cannot give adequate exercise, unless and until man gives him leave. God's justice is thus kept in a state of dependence on human folly or improbity.

Concerning the absurdity—the *simple* absurdity—of the supposition, thus much may suffice. Note now the *complex absurdity*—the *inconsistency*—involved in it. For this purpose set to work two *swearers*—with or without to each of them an *administerer*,—with or without, to each of them, a *prescriber*, an *ordainer* of the oath: two swearers, swearing, and thus respectively engaging themselves, to direct their utmost endeavours to the production of two opposite and altogether incompatible effects. By the draughts thus drawn for eventual punishment, what, according to the current theory, is the effect produced upon the Almighty? What? but that he is *compelled*, or, if that word be too plain and clear, *engaged*, to lend his power, at the same place and time, to the production of these same opposite and incompatible effects?

For the field of action, meaning the geographical field,

* If the majority of a great nation are to be kept in a state of everlasting degradation,—with probable, not to say just, cause of eventual revolt perpetually administered to it,—for what reason is it to be thus dealt with? Is it because, independently of all oaths, it is a king's duty so to govern? No: but because by an oath which he took, he swore that he would so govern: which oath taken, the consequence is, that should it happen to him to govern otherwise, God stands engaged to punish him as for perjury. If the supposed effect of an oath be any thing less than this, whence comes the fear of doing, after and notwithstanding the oath, exactly what would have been done had there been no such oath?

take for example England: for the political field, religion,—technical religion: in it place two contending religions, Catholicism and Church of Englandism: swearers and proposed actors, James and George, two contenders for the throne—what James swears is—that, in respect of wealth, power, dignity, and other good things of all sorts, the teachers and professors of the old religion shall, so far as depends upon his endeavours, be, absolutely speaking, as great as possible, and, speaking by comparison, as much greater as possible, than those of the new one:—what George swears, is—that, so far as depends upon his endeavours, the reverse of all this shall have place. According to the theory of the binding power of an oath, and the supernatural punishment attached to perjury, what is the work thus cut out for the Almighty?—To combat each religion, and at the same time and place to defend it: to combat it with one hand, to defend it with the other: to employ one person to combat it, and at the same time and place another person to defend it.

Pressed by these consequences, yet unwilling to give up altogether an instrument of such antiquity, and to which common opinion is in use to attach so much importance—"No," (says somebody) "this is going too "far: this inference about punishment is more than what "the ceremony, including the words and gestures of "which it is composed, could upon a closer view be seen "to warrant. '*So help me God,*' says the royal swearer "in the coronation oath: '*So help you God,*' says the ad-"ministerer in other cases:—what is there about punish-"men there?—Then comes the kiss given by the swearer "to the book: what is there about punishment in this "kiss?"

True, says the answer, nothing.

But among a great variety of forms, by all of which, in different ages and countries, and in particular in this age and country, an oath has been alike considered as being administered and taken, this is but one: and by all of them the effect considered as produced is of the same kind,—by all of them, that which has just been stated. Moreover, in all these cases, as often as the engagement so taken is considered as having been violated, *perjury*—or what, in the language in question, is the equivalent of that word—is the name by which such violation is designated:—the signs infinitely diversified, the thing signified every where the same:—every where either that which is above described, or nothing.

§ 2. *Mischievousness of this instrument considered in a general point of view.*

FROM mere incongruity, in this case as in any other, any inference that could be drawn, might not, when considered in a practical point of view, be regarded as having much claim to attention: from mere incongruity, that is, if so it were, that, of the institution in question, the effects, taken all together, presented a balance on the side of utility.

True: but, on inquiry, what (it is supposed) will appear clear beyond dispute, is—that of its influence the real, not to say the whole, amount is on the contrary side: to the here supposed or any other *good* purpose, its *inefficiency* complete; to *bad* purposes, in no small variety, as well as number and extent, its *efficiency* indubitable.

Of its *inefficiency*, viz. to any useful purpose,—and in particular to the purpose of securing fulfilment to any useful obligation to which in that view it is attached,—a view will be given presently.

Of the infinite variety of applications of which this instrument of government is susceptible, the only one which in a direct way bears upon the present purpose, is that which regards the subject of *evidence*. In the list of the mischiefs of which the use of it will be found productive, it is to those which result from the application made of it to this particular purpose, that the first place must accordingly be acknowledged to be due. But, the instrument being in all cases one and the same,—the use of it not being, in this particular application of it, maintainable, without being maintained in every other application that, in this country at least, continues to be made of it,—hence it is, that, in the account of its mischievous effects, to those which result from this particular application of it in its character of an *assertory—testimonial—oath*, must be added those which result from its application in the character of a *promissory oath at large*.

Before the consideration of its mischievous effects in this or that particular shape is entered upon, notice is due to an observation, which on this occasion will naturally enough be apt to present itself, as in practice it has been in use to present itself, in the character of an answer;—an answer, clearing the instrument in a great degree if not altogether, of all imputation on this score. When, in the case of this or that application of it, pure mischief is beyond dispute seen to follow from the observance of it, the oath, it is said, is in this case *void*:—absolutely null and void. In form and appearance it is an oath; but, not having the binding form of an oath, it has not the substance. This being the case, the conclusion is—that, upon the true and genuine instrument, whatsoever mischiefs may be the result of the use made of any such spurious instrument, ought not to be charged.

The oath is void!—The expression is familiar enough, but what meaning is there at the bottom of it?—The oath, this particular oath is void? *i. e.* is not really binding upon the Almighty, whom it undertakes to bind? Is this what is meant? If so, the truth of this observation must be admitted to be above dispute: for by what human instrument, under this or any other name, can omnipotence be bound? But, in regard to mischievous effects, be they what they may, it leaves the case where it found it.

By *man*—by the men upon whose agency it may come to have a bearing,—by them will it or will it not be considered—by them, let its effects have been in ever so high a degree mischievous, has it not been considered—as binding upon them?—The oath that *Jephthah* took, was it or was it not by Jephthah considered as binding upon Jephthah? The oath that Herod took, was it or was it not by Herod considered as binding upon Herod? The oath which George took, was it or was it not consi-sidered by George as binding upon George? Such are the questions that call for answer, when, whether, in speaking of it, any such words as *null* or *void* be employed or not employed in speaking of it, its effects, good and bad together, experienced and probable, come to be weighed.

"The oath," says the casuist,—"the oath which He-"rod took—was a *void* oath:"—what, in the mouth of the casuist, is the meaning of this phrase?—Either this or nothing, viz. that, in the situation of that tyrant, the casuist, had it happened to him to have taken such an oath, would not have considered himself as bound by it. May be so: but the *charger*, the fatal charger, was it the less cruelly stained by innocent blood?

"Taken in the sense in which George is supposed or "pretended to have understood it, the oath which he "took would" (says the casuist) "have been a *void* "oath." Be it so. But four millions of his own subjects, in the breast of each of whom was inclosed a soul not less precious than his own, a conscience not less entitled to consideration than his own—four millions of his own countrymen, with their posterity to the end of time—were they the less peremptorily treated in the character of an everlastingly degraded cast, composed of everlastingly dangerous adversaries? Were the hands of the sovereign less inexorably employed, in sowing the seeds of rebellion broad cast, and sharpening the axe for heads, more than could find room in many a thousand *chargers*?

Besides the irrelevancy of it, as above shown,—at the bottom of every observation, for the expression of which any such adjective as *null* or *void*, any such substitute as *nullity* is employed, an inconsistency, an irremoveable inconsistency will be found. From the ceremony and that alone, is the binding force, whatever it be that is supposed to attach on the case, derived; from the ceremony and nothing else:—and the ceremony, beneficial in any degree—pernicious in any degree in its application—the ceremony, which, except the application is all there is in the case, is it not in every case the same?

§ 3. *Its inefficiency in the character of a security against deceptious incorrectness and incompleteness in evidence.*

Of the utter inefficiency of this instrument, when employed by itself, and without either punishment or shame for its support, the demonstration, for such surely it might be made, would, for the completion of it, require more room than can here be spared.

For every thing but demonstration, the bare term *Custom-house oath*, added to the *perjurious unanimity* secured, in the case of *jurymen*, as above, by impending torture, might of themselves perhaps suffice.

It is not without that extreme reluctance, of which the causes may without much difficulty be imagined, that the necessity is here yielded to of adding *University oaths* :—English University-Statute-enforcing oaths.

When the question has been concerning a Mahometan, a Hindoo, a Chinese,—or even a Christian, if a Catholic,—great doubts have been entertained, by pious and learned Church of England men—lawyers—and non-lawyers—concerning the degree of binding force, which, in any such heterodox bosom, ought to be ascribed to the ceremony of an oath.

But, in the case of one of the two English Universities,—thence in the case of about one half of the English Church of England clergy,—the right reverend prelates not excluded,—if conduct be any proof of opinion, no room can be found for doubt. Ask what regard?—answer, Not a particle. Ask what binding force?—answer, None whatever.

In the University of Oxford, on the admission of every member, an oath is administered to him, by which, without exception, "all the statutes, privileges, and customs of the University," and for aught appears, present and future, cognoscible and uncognoscible, are promised by him to be observed *.

Of this treasure of antique wisdom,—part polished, part recast, part originally cast—nobody knows in what proportions—by the hand of Laud †,—so much as is contained in about 261 closely printed Latin pages, and which makes but a part, nor that a determinate one, of the whole body ‡, is at the same time put into the young man's hand:—what else there may be of it remaining locked up in the archives, invisible to every eye but those of the members of the governing aristocracy—the heads of houses.

Amongst the provisions in these Statutes are to be found articles in no small abundance, which, to every member without exception, are objects of continual, notorious, and open violation. Every member violates them himself, every member sees them continually violated by every other.

Of the ordinances thus violated, a great part, not to say the greater, are (it may perhaps be said) manifestly and completely useless: and accordingly the violation of them not mischievous.—Are they so indeed? For the purpose then of the argument at least, be it so: but *the inefficiency of the ceremony*, which is the only point here in question, is not the less incontestable.

Talk of Custom House oaths, when such are the Uni-

* Page 261. "*The oath at the matriculation of a scholar.* Tu fidem dabis ad observandum omnia statuta, privilegia, et consuetudines hujus Universitatis Oxon. Ita Deus te adjuvet, tactis Sacro-Sanctis Christi Evangelii."

† Laud's Diary, as referred to in his Life in the Biographia Britannica:—Dr. Newton, principal of Hertford college, in page 19 of his "University Education," London 1726, hereinafter mentioned.

‡ "Parecbolæ sive Excerpta e Corpore Statutorum Universitatis Oxoniensis . . . . In usum Juventutis Academicæ," says the title page. "Oxonii e Typographeo Clarendoniano 1794. This is the date of that which has recently been put into my hand, as the last edition extant. Of my own copy, which, at my own matriculation, was put into my hands in 1759, the date is 1756. Number of pages in the edition of 1756, 254: in that of 1794, 261.

versity oaths! Talk of merchants, when of such is the Bench of Bishops! In a Custom House, men pure from perjury must surely be to be found: so at least let us hope, were it only for the credit of those, who, in the case of universal perjury, would be the universal suborners. In a Custom House many, in the University of Oxford—pure from perjury no man—for ages has been,—or, where the swallowing the about to be continually violated oath continues to be, amongst other breaches of sincerity, the price exacted for admission, will ever be,—to be found.

In that chief nursery of Church of England piety, on the part of the rulers at least, never was *perjury* more completely unsusceptible of any such excuse as might be supposed to be afforded by *inadvertence*: on the part of the same reverend persons, in whose power it has always been, either to keep the oath or to abolish it, never was *subornation of perjury* more determinate. Not to speak of indirect, though not the less intelligible, charges,—from one of themselves*, for some thirty or forty years past, in another book, which, written by another member not only of the same University but of the same sacred function, has gone through many more editions than the Statute-book itself†,—the charge has been urged in terms

* Here follows what is said by the Rev. R. Newton, D. D. at that time Principal, in a tract, intituled, "*Hints and Statutes for the Government of Hertford College, in the University of Oxford.*" London, 1747, pp. 162, p. 98. "And for a student or scholar to take an oath at his entrance that he will observe the statutes, there can be no occasion, *if* the imposing an oath upon him for that purpose *were innocent*.... *Young* men will often break them without adverting that they do so. To them an oath to observe the statutes will be a snare." In conversation, in conduct, and in print, from some year earlier than 1725, to some year later than 1747, did this truly conscientious divine continue to give vent to the uneasiness occasioned by the load, which, ever since the year 1634, has by Archbishop Laud, in his quality of Chancellor and Legislator of this University, been laid upon all such consciences as it has found in that tabernacle, in which, wherever it has not by priestcraft or lawyercraft been extirpated, that organ of the mind will still be to be found.

† Here follows what is said in a book, intituled, "*Liberal Education, by Vicesimus Knox, M. A. late Fellow of St. John's College, Ox-*

so pointed, as to take from this repetition of it, all merit on the ground of originality, and therefore surely to save it from all reproach, not only of calumny, but of unnecessary asperity.

From the perjury thus rendered habitual and universal, ingenuity, as will be seen further on, was at an early period employed, in the endeavour to remove the *name*. But, by this very endeavour, as will also be seen, the *charge*, instead of being removed, has been but the more directly pointed, as well as the more firmly fixed.

" What ?—(it may here be said)—whatever inferences " may be found deducible from this state of things, is " this then to be one, viz. that, to the testimony deli- " vered, upon any occasion, under the sanction of an " oath, by any of the reverend, right reverend, and " other distinguished persons, at whose instance the sort " of perjury above exhibited has been constant and uni- " versal, no more regard would be due than to that of " an equal number of persons convicted of perjury, viz. of " mendacious testimony delivered in a court of justice?"

ford, in two vols. 10th edition, 1789:" to which is added, " A Letter to .... Lord North," then Chancellor.

In vol. I. p. 120, " The following," says he, " are miscellaneous passages from Dr. Newton and Mr. Amhurst : .... " To give a just account of the state of the University of Oxford, I must begin where every fresh man begins, with admission and matriculation; for so it happens, that the first thing a young man has to do there, is to prostitute his conscience, and enter himself into perjury at the same time that he enters himself into the University." Whereupon, in the same quotation, follow instances in abundance, out of others that in much greater abundance might have been adduced.

Mr. Knox, for many years master of Tunbridge school, is the person by whom, on this occasion, I consider the statement as made : who the other person was whose words he here employs, is an article of information which to the present purpose is scarcely worth obtaining : *Amhurst*, as above, is mentioned as his name : no mention of the page, or so much as of the title of the work. Whatsoever it may have given to that of the honest author, to the conscience of the Right Honourable Minister and Chancellor, to whom it was addressed, it does not appear to have given any more disturbance, than it has to that of any past or present, or seems in danger of giving to that of any future successor, not to speak of their respective *Vices*.

My answer is—By no means. Not more revolting would any such inference be upon the first mention of it, than upon examination it would be seen to be unfounded, as well as irrelevant with relation to the present purpose. What is *not* here *contended* for is—that in the instances of those by whom this useless promissory oath has thus been violated, testimony, whether delivered with or without oath, has a less chance for being pure from mendacity than in the instance of those, by whom no such oath having been taken, no such oath has been violated. What *is* here *contended for*, is—that, in those same instances if, after an assertory, if after a testimonial oath taken, testimony is pure from mendacity, such purity has for its cause—not the force of *this* instrument, but the force of those instruments, one or more or all of them, which have already been brought to view, in the general character of the *tutelary* or *improbity-restraining*, and in the particular character of the *mendacity-restraining* sanctions. What in these same instances is *denied* is—*not* the existence of veracity in the character of an effect, but the efficiency, the relative efficiency, of the instrument here in question, in the character of a cause productive of, or contributing to the production of, that effect. Fear of eventual *punishment* in most cases—fear of eventual *shame* in all cases—fear of punishment at the hand of the Almighty—these are the springs of action that have been brought to view in the character of improbity-restraining forces in general, and mendacity-restraining forces in particular. In the present case, so it is, that of these three forces, the two first at least have notoriously no application. In this case the oath is taken by every body, every body violates the oath so taken, nobody is ever punished for violating it, nobody is ever put to shame by the violation of it. And such then is the ground of the inference,—viz. that, to whatsoever object directed, whether to the prevention of transgression in any other shape, or to the prevention of transgression in the particular shape of mendacity, the instrument in question, the ceremony of an oath, is inefficient and useless.

In every case, whatsoever be the force in which the legislator puts his trust, it concerns him surely to know it for what it is: and if so indeed it were, that, by religion, such force as that sanction is in possession of is actually employed in the endeavour to deter men from transgression in the shape in question—from transgression in the shape of perjury,—it has now been seen what that force really amounts to: and then would come the question, whether, supposing that sanction really to receive support from the enormously expensive machinery which is seen to be employed in the support of it, or under the notion of giving support to it, whether the value of the support be equal to the value of the expense.

A less grating supposition will surely be, that, in the endeavour to keep men's lips pure from transgression, at least in this particular shape, the force of religious hopes and fears does *not* employ itself: but, upon this supposition, the ceremony, its inutility considered, will be parted with without reluctance: always remembered, that, even by the articles of the Church of England, the use made of it is stated—not as necessary, but simply as allowable.

§ 4. *Recognition of its inutility by Lords and Commons.*

By the House of Commons is exercised,—if, *in appearance*, relation had to the two other component branches of the sovereignty, no more than a *co-equal*, or in some respects even *inferior*, in *effect* and *experience* a universally superintending and thereby *superior*, authority in every department of government. If, in *legislation*, it possesses but one out of three shares, yet, by the exclusive origination of the measures necessary to the giving to the body politic its daily bread, that share is in effect (corruptive influence apart) rendered little less than the whole.

Over the acts, and thereby over the persons, of the possessors of the several powers belonging to the *administrative* department, the person of the monarch alone excepted, it possesses that controul and superiority which is constituted by the direct as well as exclusive right of *prosecution*, and the virtual power of *dismission*; including, to the extent of the suffering by loss of office and its emolument, the power of *punishment*: so likewise over the possessors of the powers belonging to *judicature*, with the exception of the few persons in whose instances the virtual power of dismission requires the concurrence of the House of Lords.

Be this rough outline more or less correct, on the manner more or less fit, in which these several powers are exercised, depends, day by day, not only the well-being, but the very being of the state.

On the correctness and completeness of the *conception* formed in relation to the several matters of fact, on which the acts done in the exercise of these several powers are grounded, and thence on the correctness and completeness of the mass of *evidence*, from which in each instance that conception is deduced, depends, in each instance, the propriety or impropriety, the salutariness or the mischievousness, of the exercise given to those powers.

All this while,—in so far as, concerning what a man thinks it right for him to do, any inference can be drawn from what he does,—of all those several practices, on each of which the life of the body *politic* is no less continually dependent than that of the body *natural* on respiration, not one is there to which, in the opinion of that assembly, any necessary security against deceptious incorrectness or incompleteness, is by this ceremony afforded—any useful service rendered.

Here then comes the inference—dispute it that man, by whom any the faintest colour of reason to combat it with can be found. Either by both these sets of trustees for the rest of the community, their respective trusts have on every occasion been betrayed;—betrayed by the Commons by their not assuming this power, by the Lords by their not conceding it;—or, on every occasion, to the purpose of ascertaining facts by evidence, in the opinion of both these authorities, the ceremony of an oath is needless.

The proceeding for which a ground is to be made—will it be said, that, when it is of comparatively inconsiderable importance, then indeed, the fitness of the proceeding *does* depend upon the goodness of the ground, but in the case where it is of the highest importance *not?* This and nothing less must be maintained—maintained by him by whom the justness of the above inference is stated as open to dispute.*

§ 5. *Mischiefs.*—1. *Contributing to the mendacity-licence granted by Judges.*

In the abridged work on the *Rationale of Evidence*,—in speaking of the securities for trustworthiness there mentioned in the character of true ones,—under the head of punishment, explanation was given of the *mendacity-licence*;—of the mode in which it was and is granted, and, in general terms, of the mode in which the ceremony termed *an oath* was made subservient to that flagitious purpose. On the occasion of judicial testimony, be the mendacity ever so pernicious, punishment (it has there been seen) stands in general confined to the case, in which, as a security against the practice of that vice, this ceremony had, on the occasion of the delivery of the testimony, been applied to it. In this as in other cases where prevention has been desired, by the application of punishment the effect of a *prohibition* was and is produced: in this as in other cases where prevention has been matter of indifference, or production an object of desire,

* Question concerning an object to the value of a shilling or a halfpenny—no trial of it without this sacred ceremony. Question, as in the case of the Orders in Council, between war and peace, between national starvation and life—no such security employed: no decision suspended for want of it.—What more need be said?—no thought taken for it.

by omission to apply punishment, whether the omission had for its cause design or inadvertency, the effect of a *licence* was and is produced: and, so sure as the omission has design for its cause, or observation of the effects for its accompaniment, so surely is not only the effect of a licence produced, but, in whichsoever of a variety of imaginable forms, the licence itself is in substance granted*.

* Of the aggregate mischief of the institution here in question, the judicial abuse, which in the work mentioned in the text has been designated under the appellation of *the mendacity licence*, forms so material a part, that, unless the view there given of it were here inserted, any conception that could hence be formed of it would want much of being an adequate one. As the present tract, though, if room can be found for it, designed to constitute an appendix to the abovementioned work on Evidence, is moreover designed to appear in the form of a separate publication, it has been deemed advisable to reprint in this place that part of the work on Evidence, in which the abuse here in question has been more fully delineated and explained.

It forms the fourth section of the eighth chapter, intituled, Of THE SECURITIES FOR TRUSTWORTHINESS IN EVIDENCE, and is in these words, viz.

§ 4. *Judge and Co.—False evidence rendered by them dispunishable, where profitable to themselves.—Mendacity-licence.*

Thus much as to *propriety*:—for *practice*, learned ingenuity has discovered and pursued a more convenient course.

Under the English, not to speak of other systems of technical procedure, by means of the command, so easily, when indirectly, exercised by *power* over *language*, an expedient was found for rendering mendacity punishable or unpunishable at pleasure. In the person of a party litigant, or a witness, when it was to be rendered *punishable*, the allegation or statement was called *evidence*; and, to mark is as such, a particular *ceremony*—the ceremony of an *oath*—was made to accompany the delivery of it. When it was to be rendered *dispunishable*, it was *not* to be called *evidence*:—it was to be called *pleading*—*pleadings*—any thing but *evidence*;—and the *ceremony* was to be carefully kept from touching it.

At this time of day, few tasks would naturally be more difficult, than that of satisfying the English lawyer, that *pleadings* not upon oath—that any thing, in a word, which in legal use has been carefully and customarily distinguished from evidence, can with propriety be termed *evidence*. But though, thanks to his ingenuity, so it is that pleadings—all pleadings at least—are not evidence in *name*, yet so it is, that every thing that goes by the name of *pleading*, is evidence, in effect. All testimonial *evidence* is *statement*—*narration*—*assertion*: every thing that goes by the name of *pleadings*, is so too. Of *evidence*, the use, and sole use, is to command decision:—by *pleadings* decision is

When, for the purpose of revenue, an occupation or transaction not meant to be prohibited is thus clogged by a licence, money, with the effect though not under

commanded, and *that* in cases to a vast extent, and in continual recurrence, and with a degree of *certainty* altogether denied to *evidence.*

To the purpose of imposing on the adverse party the obligation of going on with the suit, the contents of every instrument included under the name of *pleadings*, how replete soever with manifest falsehood, are taken for true, and as such, without the *name*, have the *effect* of *evidence*. This effect (it may be said) is but provisional: but definitively, to the purpose of giving to the suit a termination favourable to the party by whom the instrument is exhibited,—to the purpose of producing a decision—a decision as favourable to him as could be produced by any thing to which the name of *evidence* has been left,—to the purpose of producing the self-same decision, which, by evidence, supposing it believed, would be produced—it *has* the effect—not simply of evidence, but of *conclusive* evidence:—the party who fails to meet the instrument in question,—by some instrument, which, at the next step that, on the other side, ought, in the appointed course to follow it,—loses his cause.

Of this eventually-conclusive evidence, the power, it may be said, cannot be great, since,—by so proper and simple an operation, as that of exhibiting the corresponding counter-instrument, the party, to whose prejudice the conclusion would operate,—gets rid of it. Simple enough, yes: but instances are but too abundant, in which the operation, simple as it is, is impracticable—foreknown to be impracticable. To the performance of the operation, money is necessary: and on that side—money being by the other side known not to be forthcoming—what is thereby known is, that the exhibition of the counter instrument is *not* practicable. It is accordingly because foreknown to be impracticable, that the operation is thus called for: for which purpose, falsehood, the most barefaced falsehood, is admitted to serve, admitted by those judges to whom its quality is no secret:—admitted with exactly the same composure as if it were known to be the strictest truth.

Thus it is, that under favour of the mendacity-licence thus established, every man, who, being to a certain degree opulent, has, or desires to take, for his adversary, a man to a certain degree less opulent, has it in his power, whether on the plaintiff's side, or on the defendant's side, to give, to his juridically-delivered allegations, by what name soever denominated—*pleadings* or any other,—the effect of *evidence:*—the effect, not only of evidence, but of *conclusive* evidence.

And thus it is, that by the forbearance—the astute forbearance—to give, to the security afforded by punishment, the extent necessary to justice, mendacity is generated and cherished, injustice, through misdecision, produced:—the evils opposite to the *direct* ends of justice produced, by means of the evils opposite to the *collateral* ends of justice.

the name of *purchase-money*, is exacted for it, and that money is applied to the use of the community at large, through the medium and by the hands of Government.

Among lawyers, and more especially among English lawyers, so commodiously, and thence so universally, is *custom* accepted as an adequate substitute to *reason*—so unprecedented is it for a man to trouble himself with any such thought, as, in regard to any of the established torments, out of which his comforts are extracted, what, in point of utility and justice, may have been the ground for the establishing of them—or so much as, whether they have, or ever had, any such ground at all—that, at the first mention, a question to any such effect will be apt to present itself to them, as no less novel, than idle and absurd. But concerning *judgment by default*, and every thing that is equivalent to it *,—be it in a House of Commons,—be it in a House of Lords,—be it in any other place,—should any such misfortune happen to him, as to feel himself under a necessity of finding something in the character of a reason to give, in answer to the question—why it is that *judgment by default* is made to follow upon default, his reason would be this or nothing, viz. that in this case, on the defaulting side, *want of merits* is inferred; and not only so, but that it is from the allegations contained in the instrument last-delivered on the other side—it is from that, and nothing else, that the inference is deduced.

At the same time, that which, be he who he may, is well known to him—or at least, but for his own wilful default, would be known to him—that which he has always in his hands the means of knowing—means beyond comparison more ready than any which are possessed by the vast multitude, who at the instance of his tongue, and by the power of his hand, are so incessantly and remorselessly punished,—punished for not knowing that which it has so diligently and effectually been rendered impossible they should know, is—that, in the case of an average individual, the chances *against* the truth of the conclusion, thus built and acted upon, are many to *one*.

To be assured of this, all that a man has to do on the one side of the account, is to look at the average, or even at the minimum amount of the costs on both sides, which, on each side, a party subjects himself to the eventual burthen of,—or though it were at those on one part only;—on the other side of the account, at the annual amount of what an average individual of the labouring class (beyond all comparison the most numerous class)—or even though it were an average individual of the aggregate of all classes, the very highest not excluded—has for the whole of his possible expenditure. This

* [*Equivalent to it*] Examples—In Common Law practice, *Judgment as in case of a nonsuit*: in Equity practice, taking of the bill *pro confesso*, in case of what is called *contempt*; for,—when, by the ruin of his fortunes, and consequent inability to pay the appointed price for a chance of justice, a man has been reduced to the lowest pitch of humiliation,—*contempt*, the offspring of *pride*, is imputed to him; and it is for this *pride* that he is punished:—punished, by being excluded from that chance.

In the case of the licence here brought to view under the name of the mendacity-licence—(the judicial or testimonial mendacity-licence) a licence by which, through the

comparison made, then it is, that any man may see, whether, by forbearance to *go on* with an existing suit, at any stage, on *either* side,—whether, on the *plaintiff's* side, by forbearance to *commence* a suit,—any preponderant probability be afforded, of what is called a *want of merits*.

Of two all-pervading masses of instances, in which, throughout the whole system of technical judicature, conclusions, having been built, are continually acted upon,—acted upon by men, to whom, one and all, the *promises* on which those conclusions are built, and thence the conclusions themselves, are—or, without their own wilful default, would be—known to be false, this is the first, for the mention of which the occasion has here happened to present itself.

Under the head of *non-observance of formalities*, a failure considered as being, or at least dealt with as if it were, *evidence*—evidence conclusively probative of unfairness on the part of a contract, or spuriousness on the part of an instrument of contract—under this other head, mention of another instance will come to be made in the chapter on *pre-appointed evidence*.

Nullification,—to which belong conjugates and quasi conjugates much too abundant to be here collected,—*null, void, bad, quash, set aside*, and so forth—*nullification* is the name given to the factitious engine of iniquity, by which the sort of effect here spoken of, is in both instances produced. Instruments and operations of judicial *procedure*—*contracts* and *instruments of contract*—whatsoever has been the *subject* to which it has been applied, *lawyer's profit* is what the machinery will be found to have had exclusively for its *object*, *lawyercraft* for its inventor and constructor, iniquity and misery for its *effects*.

By encouragement as well as impunity thus given to mendacity,—if it be on the plaintiff's side, the number of suits is made to receive that addition, which is brought to it by those in which the dishonesty—the *mala fides*, as the phrase is—is on the plaintiff's side: by the like boon bestowed on the defendant's side, the like addition is made to the number of those to which *continuance* is given by dishonesty on the defendant's side.

See more to this purpose under the head of *Oath*.

On all these occasions, partner and accomplice in the fraud on one side of the cause, in the oppression on the other, the judge, as well as his collaborators, extracts emolument out of the mendacity thus produced under the name of *pleadings*,—the mendacious evidence thus suborned is all in writing,—and the mass of writing is a mine of fees*.

* To quote or refer to the instances in which profit-yielding mendacity is thus generated, would be to quote or refer to the whole contents of the several law books, in which, under the name of *books of practice*, for the use and benefit of the members of the profession, the course of judicial procedure is delineated.

medium of wilful falsehood, a man was, and is, allowed and empowered to work injustice to an unlimited amount, the tax being imposed by the authority of the Judges, the produce of it was and is divided, though in casual and not distinctly discernible proportions, between themselves, their subordinates, and other their confederates, in various situations and of various denominations, partners in the traffic of justice and injustice.

Nothing could be more artful, nothing was ever more successful, than this their scheme of policy: without any of the infamy, they derived all the advantage of encouragement given to the profit-yielding vice: and, by the impenetrable secrecy by which it was concealed, the value of the profit, so far from being diminished, was proportionably increased.

To the purpose of this disguise the ceremony was in an eminent degree serviceable. If, for producing the effect of a licence, no such ceremony being in use, no instrument had been employable but punishment, undisguised punishment,—employable, *viz.* by the direct and manifest forbearance to apply to mendacity, on *one* occasion, that punishment which on *another* occasion, and *that* not presenting any greater demand, was applied to it,—the device might have been too transparent to be hazarded. But when, in the character of an intermediate instrument, the ceremony, with its terrors, was called in, and set to work, its mysteriousness served as a curtain, behind which the eyes of the awe-struck multitude were terrified from any attempt to penetrate.

What was conspicuous enough, and to every eye, was the assistance lent to justice in most of the instances in which this sanction was employed:—for, inefficient as on these occasions it would have been of itself,—and, as on every occasion, in which it is without support from shame or punishment it is found to be,—yet, when backed by punishment, as on these occasions care was taken that it should be, it derived from the punishment such support as in each case it was in the nature of the punishment, such as it was, to give. What *was* seen, and by every body, was, therefore, the assistance that, by this instrument, was lent to justice, in the cases in which it was applied. What was *not* seen by any body, those excepted whose interest it was not to speak of it, was the debility—the state of prostrate debility—in which the hand of justice was left, in every case in which this necessary armature was not given to it.

Had neither oath nor punishment attached upon any part of the mixt mass of evidence, shame would, in case of falshood, and with a degree of force proportioned to what was understood to be its degree of mischievousness, have attached upon every such polluted part. But, when the distinction that was made was to such a degree conspicuous, the two combined sanctions (the only two which are under the direct command of government) being to one part of the mass applied in combination, while to the other part neither of them was applied, shame could not in the unmarked part find any sure ground to fix upon. Unless it were the issuing, in express terms, a declaration pronouncing falshood blameless, neither licence nor so much as approbation could, by these official guardians of public morals, have in any other way been given to this their cherished and richly profitable vice.

Not that even of declarations, little if any thing less express and open, examples but too frequent might not be found. A penitent criminal confessing his guilt, the judge urging him to deny it:—contests of this sort may be seen in print, between a falshood-hating felon and a falshood-loving judge: and, lest the poison of mendacity should not with sufficient certainty and effect work its way into the public breast, Hypocrisy has thus been seen stirring in the honey of humanity to sweeten it*.

* Under the French system of regular procedure, the range of the mendacity-licence was still more extensive than under the English. Those incidental or interlocutory instruments, applications, and other operations, which, under the English system, require, to give them effect, testimony delivered *upon oath* (viz. in the shape of a ready-written *affidavit*) were, under the French system, with little or no exception, made, and performed, and effect given to them *without oath*.

§ 6. *Mischief 2. Weakening in various ways the efficiency of the Laws.*

VARIOUS are the occasions on which, various the ways in which, the effect of this ceremony has been to confuse the texture, and enervate the effective force of the whole body of the laws.

Were the force of which it deprives the arm of justice no other force than its own, the mischief, as already intimated, would be scarce worth taking into account. But the performance of this ceremony having been rendered necessary,—in some cases to the application of an adequate lot of punishment in case of the delivery of mendacious testimony,—in other, and indeed in most cases, and these in the greater number, to the very attempt to extract or receive the testimony,—hence it is, that throughout its whole field of legal action, by the mere non-application of this *stimulus*, the arm of the law is left in a palsied and inefficient state.

In the 864 small-typed pages of a quarto volume (*Ravaut—Procédure Civile du Palais*) not the least trace of an *affidavit*, or any thing that, in respect of *oath* or *punishment*, could have been calculated to answer the purpose, could be discovered.

The consequence was—that, for protracting litigation, lies, so they were but in writing, were, by French, uttered and received for truth with still less reserve, if possible, than by English justice. Still more perhaps than here, confusion was thickened, and litigation lengthened, by diversity of Courts and appeals.

The pace of English Common Law was out-lingered in the Westminster Halls of France. By any such distinction as that between *Common Law* and *Equity*, with different though confederated sets of shops for the sale of them, the understandings of mankind have no where been insulted but in England. But, derived as it was from the same Roman source, French *Common Law*, such was its dilatoriness and predatoriness, might, like the Scottish, be said to be all *Equity*. What was worse, even their *criminal* law was in this respect all *Equity*. Of the causes reported in the *Causes Célèbres*, the average duration was found to be about *six years*. There, as here, the mass of writing was a gold mine to Judges and their creatures.

Linguet (Plaidoyers vii. 118. Leloir's case) mentions as one of the particularities of that case, that, while, of such part of the costs as went to pay the advocate and the attorney, the amount was

I. In the first place may be mentioned *exclusion*—the virtual exclusion, put by it upon the testimony of a numerous class of men. And what men? men whose distinguishing characteristic is—that, in their instance a more than ordinary degree of sensibility to the force of the religious sanction, is, by the most unequivocal tokens, put out of dispute. Before these pages are at an end, the absurdity of any such exclusion will, it is hoped, be rendered plain, if any thing can be rendered plain, even in the case of the most flagrant and manifest improbity and untrustworthiness:—*here* the object on which the stigma is made to strike is that class of men which stands most eminently distinguished for trustworthiness.

Swear not at all, says Jesus: at least in as far as to his biographer Matthew, credence may in this point be ventured to be given. "Swear not at all," says Jesus: and as if, unless inculcated and enforced by reasons, a precept so simple should escape from remembrance, reasons are subjoined. Professing himself a religionist of the religion of Jesus,—an obeyer of the ordinances of Jesus,—and of all the ordinances attributed to Jesus,—not

no more than 60 livres, that part that went to the Judges, being under the names of *Epices* and *Vacations*, paid to them for *l'arrêt* (viz. the judgment or a copy of it) was more than 400 livres. Under the French edition of Rome-bred procedure, these costs of the *arrêt* corresponded to the costs of the *extraction of the decreet* in the Scotch edition. It was among the undisguised endeavours of the professional assistants of the parties to save their clients from judicial depredation in this shape.

Adam Smith (Chapter *on the expence of Justice*) proclaims the purity of the French Judges. Pure they were, it seems true enough; but as their brethren in England were pure also: pure, where impurity would have been *dangerous* to the hands that dabbled in it; impure, where it was safe.

On the other hand, of natural procedure, out of the pale of which, what is called *justice* has no where in design been any thing better than regulated pillage, but with effects beyond comparison more grievous than those of pillage to the same pecuniary amount, the range was much more extensive *there* than *here*.

Witness the judicatories called *Consular Courts*.

Of the nuisance called *Equity*, a lover of *justice* will be glad to know, that in the American United States she has already in a great degree rid herself, as of so many other English nuisances.

seeing any ordinance more clear or precise than this, a Quaker refuses to disobey it. For this refusal it is, that, between Church and State matters are so ordered, that, in a case which has afforded no other witness than such as are of this persuasion, justice, criminal justice at least, is deprived of all evidence: licence being thereby granted, to all such crimes as from time to time it shall happen to any man to feel himself disposed to commit (other persons out of the question) upon the bodies, or in the presence, of any number of Quakers.

In England this same religion has been adopted. Adopted? but how?—Exactly with those same reservations, with which a Bill is at its first introduction adopted in the House of Commons; viz. with liberty of making amendments:—amendments omissive, interpolative, substitutive:—amendments of all sorts, and in all cases:—and in all cases to such effect, as the convenience of that class of men, by whose convenience every thing is regulated, was found to require.

In regard to some of its clauses, as where *poverty*, or *equality*, or *non-resistance* are ordained, the amendment made has been of the *omissive* kind. In the present instance, for the purpose here in question, it has been of the *interpolative* kind: an amendment for giving admission to such oaths, as, for purposes such as those above described, it should be found convenient to administer: to administer, amongst other occasions on the occasion of the delivery of judicial testimony.

What is certain is—that by Jesus, any such exception is not, by any one of his four biographers, represented as having been made.—Not made by him? and what then? It is of the number of those, which, though he did not make, he ought to have made*.

* At a time of pretended toleration, a statute was passed, authorising the admission of a Quaker's testimony without oath: but, lest complication and confusion should not be thick enough, confining the indulgence to cases termed *civil* cases to the exclusion of cases termed *criminal* cases. Distinct enough, the two words: but between the things themselves where is the line of distinction to be found? In the nature of the case itself?—No: but, as usual under

2. Not so much as the profession of rendering justice being to be made unless the performance of this ceremony be duly accomplished, thereupon comes more complication, more law learning, more doubts, more business.

A Jew's oath what shall it be? Must the hat be *off* or *on?* and if *on*, what shall in law be deemed and taken to be a hat? and the book what must it be? and in what language?

Jew or Christian, what is it that shall be kissed? What if, instead of the book, it be the thumb that receives the salute? what if to a book with the Song of Solomon in it, by *astutia* or *laches* of the clerk, those of Rochester be found to have been substituted? With such an instrument could a man commit perjury?

In Westminster Hall, when a man takes an oath which is said to be administered *by* a Judge or certain Judges, the Judge or Judges—must they be there or may they be not there?—Not many years ago the writer of this was sworn in this way to the truth of a mass of testimony before a learned Judge, who was any where but there. From beginning to end suppose it wilful falshood, was any of it perjury?

The Mahometan—in his system of imposture does the ceremony find the necessary virtue? does it in the still more extravagant imposture of the Hindoo? in the religion or the no-religion of the Chinese is that magic to be found, which in case of profanation draws down with such unerring certainty the ever obsequious vengeance of the Church of England God, by whom all such magic stands prohibited in terms as plain as it is in the power of language to provide? In this or that false religion suppose this ceremony to be misperformed. In

Judge-made law, in the treatment which happens to have been bestowed upon it. In a civil case millions may be included in the stake; in a criminal case, one shilling may be the amount of it: and the same case is either *civil*, or *criminal*, or both, according to the form given to the mass of absurd mendacity which a man is forced to allow his lawyers to join in the utterance of, before he is permitted to take his chance for that which is called *justice*.

the Hindoo religion for example, in which, as exquisitely turned as if it had been in Westminster Hall, the whole mass of ceremonies is a widow's cruise of nullities?

3. As often as a new statute is passed, creative of new offences—and to such novelties not a year but gives birth by dozens,—if to any judicatory other than the regular—if to Justices of the Peace, for example, one or more, as usual, cognizance of the offence be given, power must by fresh words be given for the performance of this ceremony. Here then may be seen one of the host of causes, from whose hydropic virtue the needless and endless unwieldiness of the body of the law, and the impossibility of knowing, and consequently of doing, that which man is predestinated to be legally plundered and punished for not doing, receives its daily increase.

The empowering formulary is it omitted?—This is what has sometimes happened. Deprived of this necessary support, down tumbles the paper edifice, and with it perish the hundreds or thousands of pounds that have been spent in rearing it*.

4. Exists there a case in which, be the Judge who he may, it rests with him, in collecting the information, to perform or not perform the ceremony as he pleases? Here then is despotism: here opens a door to safe corruption,—punition or impunity being attached to mendacity, according as it is the one or other that is heard called for by the sinister purpose.

5. Where, for the creation of it, the security, such as it is, requires on every occasion the interposition of human agency, it stands necessarily exposed to all those accidents, as well as to all those abuses, to which the application of human power stands exposed.

* Morning Chronicle, Wednesday, 9th Dec. 1812.
"House of Lords, 8th Dec. Insolvent Debtors.
"Lord Ellenborough presented a bill to amend and enlarge the powers of the Insolvent Act of last Session. His Lordship stated that &c. . . . . It was also proposed to give in express terms, to the Court constituted by the Barristers so appointed, the power of administering an oath, a power which had only been given by implication in the Act of last Session."

Where the oath is the security, for the application of it there must be, as above, either a magistrate, or some other functionary, empowered *quoad hoc* to execute the office of a magistrate. But, unless by a casual charity not worth reckoning upon, the magistrate will not, still less the quasi magistrate, join in the ceremony, without his fee. To those whose business with the law is to make it, and if they please to execute it, the fee is nothing. But to those whose business with the law, made or not made, is to obey it,—to the greater part of *them* at least,—the fee is something: half of what a man has to subsist himself and family upon for a day is always something to him, especially if on that day he have no work.

If, on the part of the Justice of Peace, or, according to the occasion, the Master Extraordinary in Chancery (for such is the title worn by the country attorney, when decked out in this one red feather from the magistrate's crest)—if, on the part of this regularly commissioned possessor of power over the Almighty, either inclination, (relation being had to the individual by whom, the occasion on which, and the person or persons for whose benefit the testimony is proposed to be delivered)—either inclination or ability be deficient, thereupon comes in another source of vexation, nor that a very limited one. Neither the ordinary justice, nor the extraordinary master, can be any more *obliged* to receive testimony, than, when it is in the *affidavit* shape, the proposed witness can be to deliver it: and if, in the breast of the only Extraordinary Master, whose abode is known to be within half a day's journey of the proposed deponent or answer-making defendant, so it be that, in regard to witness or party, it is more blessed to give than to receive—to give vexation than to receive a shilling,—the consequences may more speedily be imagined than expressed.

6. In the times of William the Third, amongst other driblets of sham reform, a show was made, of substituting, to a certain extent, the purity of natural to the pravity of technical procedure. Under the name of ARBITRATORS, parties were empowered to choose their

Judges: and, to the decisions pronounced by such Judges, upon application made to one of the great shops in Westminster Hall, the force of law was to be sold at an under price *.

The show was made:—was it any thing, and if any thing how much, better than a show?

In giving jurisdiction by a fresh law to a Justice or Justices out of sessions, that which to no one man of law, in or out of Parliament, could have been unknown, was —that unless for administering oaths to witnesses power were given by an express clause, the law would be without effect. In this act, with all its fine professions, no such power was given: and why not?—the answer is already seen. Where was ever that Justice of Peace, by whom, for the purpose here in question as well as any other, the Judge's part might not, as well as by a Daniel, have been acted in this ceremony? Where is the Justice of Peace's wife by whom it might not be as well acted as by her husband?

Not to speak of Clergymen, of whom each parish ought to contain at least one—and to whom for such a function there could not consistently have been a shadow of objection,—what Attorney is there.—who, not being unfit to continue on the roll, would be otherwise than fit for the pronouncing of the words in question, seeing the book kissed, and signing his name?—Fit? Yes:—nor less so than, for the application of this same ceremony to testimonial instruments collected under the authority of the Chancery Court, the same Attorney would be, if dubbed for the purpose, (as, on paying his fees, any Attorney may be) Master Extraordinary in Chancery, as above?

Here there is another instance—nor that a scantily extensive one—in which this instrument of priestcraft has

* At an expence the amount of which is among the secrets that might be worth generally knowing, the award is made *a rule of court:* this having, to the purposes of *execution*, an effect analogous to that of a *judgment*, the delay, vexation, and expence of the proceedings by which the judgment would otherwise have been preceded, are, as to such share of those evils as would have been produced in the court of technical procedure, in so far saved.

been made an instrument of deceit, hypocrisy, and mischief, in the hands of lawyercraft. Suppose no such ceremony—suppose, in manner as mentioned below, that, by an all-comprehensive provision, punishment, according to the nature of the mischief, attached, as of course, upon all mendacity, uttered upon a legal occasion, to a legal purpose,—in such case, the remedy, if not by other devices defrauded of its pretended object, would, instead of the sham remedy that it is, have been a real one*.

7. By the House of Commons, to whatsoever subject its powers are directed, for obtaining the information, whatsoever it be, on which, in the exercise of those powers, it grounds itself, whatsoever is done is done without the assistance of this ceremony.

For security against deceptious incorrectness and incompleteness, the means remaining in its hands consist

* True it is, that at present,—under an official custom, the commencement of which might be matter of curiosity at least, if not of use, in furtherance (as it would naturally be said) of the object of this statute, the three great common law justice shops in Westminster Hall have been, and continue to be, generous enough (fees being duly paid) to lend out—a partner or a journeyman as it may happen—for the performance of this ceremony; the person, whose testimony is to be delivered to the arbitrators, being taken by an attorney, to the court or one of its offices, and there sworn, a Judge being present, viz. either in fact or—what, but for the imposture, would be quite as well—in law.

But,—besides that not only the officer must on this occasion have his fee, but the attorney, by whom this witness is ushered to the office and the solemnity conducted, another, and if any, a much greater fee,—how efficient soever the Act may thus have been rendered within the limits of the metropolis and its vicinity, what, unless it be once or twice a-year for one or two days, at an assize-town, does it amount to any where else?—In pretence it was designed for the benefit of "*Merchants*:"—out of London are there no merchants? In pretence it was designed for "*Merchants and others*:"—out of London are there neither *Merchants* nor *others*?

Even this driblet of relief finds more perhaps than a counterbalance, in an abuse to which this same Act has given, if not birth, increase: the service I mean which, at an enormous increase of expence, it renders, in the character of a cloak, to the continuance given to the *forms* of Jury trial, in cases where the substance not only *is*, but is acknowledged to be, impossible. Of this abuse an exemplification may be seen in Scotch Reform, p. 76.

of that *shame*, which in case of detected and exposed mendacity takes place of itself, and the punishment which, under the name of *commitment for contempt*, attaches in case of an order made for that purpose. But as to the shame, be the delinquent who he may, the circle within which are included those by whose judgment delinquency is pronounced, and by that declaration punished, is in general comparatively a very narrow one: and, as to the punishment as for contempt, being in its duration limited to the life of the parliament, the consequence is, that from the birth to the death of the assembly, the maximum of punishment is a continually decreasing quantity, till at last being reduced to 0, mendacity, to whatsoever subject applied, obtains in this way too a licence:—a licence at the hands of *Time*.

§ 7. *Mischief 3. Bewildering and enslaving the consciences of Jurymen.*

UNDER the head of *punishment*, in the case of a witness, but principally in the case of a party, who by the admission or extraction of his testimony is in that respect considered and treated on the footing of a witness, it has been seen in what way, by an artful use made of the ceremony of an oath, means were found for producing or repressing mendacity at pleasure.

Thus far, and in these instances, the purpose admitted at least, if it did not absolutely require, that the ceremony should be regarded as binding—should be the object of real and efficient, as well as universal awe and reverence.

In the instance of another and infinitely narrower class of persons, the like purpose required that it should—this self same ceremony should—be considered and treated on the footing of an empty form:—that it should stand divested of all influence.

This was the class of *Jurymen:*—the assemblage of twelve unlearned individuals, in whose name, in certain cases, what in English-bred law is done in the way of judicature is entered as done.

So to order matters, that to one and the same individual, with no other difference than that of the individual occasion, and the station occupied by him on that occasion, one and the same ceremony should be an object of awe and of contempt, might, upon the naked mention of it, seem a problem too difficult for human ingenuity so much as to attempt the solution of. The solution of it will be seen however to have been not only attempted but accomplished: always remembered, that in whatever case any real and practical effect has been produced, produced—in appearance by the *ceremony*,—in that case *shame*, or *punishment*, or both, may be seen at the back of it: and, on the other hand, that where its influence will be seen to amount to nothing, so it is, that, in this case, the ceremony has found no such extraneous force to give support to it.

The problem all along was to this effect—so to order matters that mendacity should be unrestrictedly practised or punished,—according as the unrestrained practice or the punishment of it should be most subservient to the private interest of the Judge and his fellow-labourers; and, to this end, that, in relation to this vital part of morality, in such confusion should men's conceptions on this subject be kept involved, as to take for the standard of right and wrong, the practice of the Judge, as determined by the sinister interest of the Judge:—and that accordingly, whensoever mendacity were punished by him it should be considered as *immoral*,—whenever left by him unpunished, indifferent,—whenever encouraged or compelled by him, either indifferent or *meritorious*.

To render the confusion the thicker and more irremediable, a conception—and persuasion—that was to be rendered universally prevalent, was,—that the practice of immorality in this shape was—throughout the whole course of judicial procedure, necessary to the purposes of justice: in pursuance of which principle, matters have accordingly been so ordered, that in the instance of that class of judicial officers, (viz. *Jurymen*, whose part in the administration of justice is the object of the warmest share of popular favour and attachment,) mendacity should have been rendered an unavoidably incident accompaniment, of every thing that was done under the sacred name of justice.

At a period, which seems even to have preceded the use made of the ceremony in the character of a security for veracity in the mouth of a witness or a party,—at this early period a barbarian theology had led the rulers of nations to place their trust in this same ceremony, in the instance of public functionaries in general, in the character of a security for official probity at large:—and in particular, in the case of functionaries of the judicial order, including as well those of the professionally learned and permanent class, as those their unlearned, their occasional, and ever-changing assessors.

In the cases as yet mentioned, the expedient, by which the power of licensing falsehood was acquired, consisted in keeping out of the reach of the ceremony, the statements to which it was desired that the licence should extend itself. If over the ceremony itself the power of the man of law could find means to extend itself, in so much that, at his pleasure, it should be considered as binding or not binding, the punishment of the *religious*, as well as that of the *moral*, sanction being, at his pleasure, felt, or not felt, as attaching in case of violation,—he would, to the extent of such power, possess himself of a species of empire, not inferior to any which even the priest had been able to create for himself.

Fortunately for this enterprise, in the very operation by which alone this branch of authority was exercised, unthinking barbarism had suffered to be involved a cluster of declarations* which, they being in every case

* [*cluster of declarations*] consisting of the several virtual declarations made by the several Jurymen in and by their respective consents given to the verdict.

The habitual mendacity necessarily involved in the pretended unanimity so uselessly and wantonly necessitated, seems too manifest to require or even admit of proof.

that, with respect to the propriety of the decision, left any difference of opinion, necessarily untrue,—necessitated, in an equal degree of frequency, the profanation of the ceremony.

Of the only course, by which profanation would be avoidable, torture, terminating in death, having, under cover of the same barbaric darkness, been rendered the inevitable result,—and reliance upon a man's own opinion,—upon the suffrage of his own conscience,—being thus rendered morally impossible;—what, in the situation of Juryman, could a simple man do, to save himself from the wrath to come? Conscience, which in such cases catches at every straw, found for the burthen a proffered support in the stronger and well disciplined conscience of the Judge.—With this burthen, whatever it was, the learned conscience, as often as suited with convenience, was found ready, as of course, to charge itself:—and thus it was, that, by rendering the sacred ceremony an object of universal and necessary contempt, the man of law acquired, over the decision of Juries, a sort and degree of mastery, such as, under any mode of suffrage that would have admitted of an escape from perjury, would never have been attainable.

So many oaths, so many *nets*, in which conscience was perpetually liable to be entangled: but, on so easy a condition as that of a man's pronouncing a short word or two, and thinking nothing about the matter, a learned conscience was always at hand to cut the cords.

The violation of the ceremony, and of the obligation supposed or pretended to have been created by it, having thus been rendered habitual and universal, its impotence in the character of a *check* upon the Judge,—its unfitness for any thing but a *cloak* to him,—followed of course.

The ceremony being considered as the only security against mendacity, and a licence for the practice of that vice being considered as being effectually, though indirectly, included, in every arrangement by which the application of the ceremony was forborne; the habitual profanation of the ceremony having, at the same time, been rendered indispensably necessary to the exercise of the powers of judicature,—in a word, to what was called the administration of justice—no particular instance of the like profanation could, on any consistent ground of reason, find, in the breasts of the violators, any sentiment of repugnance.

But the looser the obligation sat upon them, the more ready, at the call of the living oracle, under any the slightest impulse of sinister interest, in whatever shape, —power, reputation *, or even momentary ease,—would each man be to shake it off.

On condition of earning it by these means, a virtual power of *pardon* has accordingly, in cases to no inconsiderable extent, been in effect imparted to Juries:—and, lest, in the shape of *power* alone, the encouragement, held out to misdecision in this shape, should not be of itself sufficient, *reputation* in the shape of the praise of *humanity* has been occasionally added †.

Plowing in confusion and perplexity, to prepare the soil for the planting of obsequiousness,—such is the husbandry, which with so brilliant a success has been practised in the field of religion:—such is the husbandry which with no less indisputable, though less observed success, has been practised in the field of law and judicature.

* Hence it is, that, in matters of *libel* for example, where, there not being any *real law*, there can not be any *real transgression*, and where, there not being any real transgression, conviction never has had, nor, till real law shall have created delinquency, and defined transgression, ever can have, any sufficient warrant,—to so happy a state of ductility has the conscience of the Jury-box been moulded, that, unless by some rare and never to be looked for casualty, prosecution and conviction—would (were it not for the intervening costs, by which trial is rendered an additional punishment,) be in effect and virtue undistinguishable.

† Example—Encouragement given to Juries, to counteract the declared intention of the Legislature, and dispense with the capital part of the appointed punishment, by attributing upon their oaths to *any number* of guineas stolen a value under that of *two* guineas. In the case of *goods*, this under valuation is continual: and, even in case of guineas—a case which admits of no possibility of unintentionality in the misstatement—examples of this mode of valuation have not been wanting.

§ 8. *Mischief* 4. *Giving aid and force to the enterprises of malefactors.*

The application made of the ceremony of an oath, to the purpose of securing observance of mischievous engagements of all kinds, has in all places and all times been too notorious to stand in need of exemplification. In the preceding instances, the hands in which, in the character of an instrument of evil, it has been brought to view, are the hands of government:—hands at any rate in which this or that portion of the powers of government has been lodged. In the present instance the hands in which in that same character it remains to be brought to view are such as, on one account or another—in a word on any account,—come under the denomination of *criminal* ones: the purposes to which it is applied by them being for example of the nature of rebellion, sedition, or mischief, or depredation, perpetrated or attempted, in the two last mentioned cases, on an extensive scale.

When, of the complicated mass of mischief of which this ceremony is productive, the branch here in question is brought to view, an answer is ready:—applied to such purposes, the oath is *null* and *void*.—Null and void, yes: but of this nullity, this invalidity, what is the meaning? This and this only, viz. that in the mind of any one of a few and still fewer writing men, by none of whom would any such engagement be ever taken, it would not, if taken, be considered as being of the number of those by which he ought to hold himself bound:—in a word that it ought not to be considered as binding.—It ought not?—true—but is it not? To the question, what are the actual effects of a thing, a suggestion concerning what ought to be its effects is—not an answer but a subterfuge.

Employ not the abuse as an argument against the use —says a wide extending fallacy, by which much confusion, much deception, much mischief has been produced. By the *use* of a thing are meant its good effects; by the *abuse* its bad effects. What? in taking account of the effects of a thing, are you to omit all the bad ones? In taking account of profit and loss, are you to omit all the items on one side?

Meantime the plain truth is—that not only a natural but a preponderant tendency to serve the purpose of abuse is of the essence of the principle: The principle is—that, independently of any demand, which, on the ground of the principle of *utility*, an act presents for punishment,—be the act what it may—good, bad, or indifferent,—fire, stolen as it were from heaven, may in this way be obtained, and employed to punish it. This, or nothing, is what is assumed and contained in the notion of the binding force of an oath.

Not but that, even supposing the nullity of the ceremony universally understood, criminal engagements—engagements for any such criminal purposes as above—might be, and, under the stimulus of the same inducements, might with reason be expected to be, entered into, as in time past. True: but, of the actually binding force, with which those engagements have been wont to be attended, so much, whatsoever it might be, as depended upon and would have been brought into action by the ceremony, would, by the abolition or universally acknowledged insignificance of the ceremony, be cut off;—be kept from applying itself to the ceremony. That hitherto on the occasion of any such mischief-brewing confederacy, the ceremony has in general been considered as possessed of, and about to operate with, such binding force, is matter of experience, since on occasions such as those in question it has, in point of fact, been called in and employed.

Of all the drugs that are in use to be employed in the way of medicine, there is not perhaps one, which might not in the way of poison be made to operate with a murderous effect. From hence does any sufficient reason result for the prohibition of the use of any of those drugs?—No:—but of any known drug suppose it ascertained to be no less apt to be employed with effect to the purpose of destroying life than to that of restoring health,—while, with reference to every beneficial purpose to which it is supposed applicable, others, known to be applicable with equal effect, without being equally applicable to its deleterious purposes, are with equal facility obtainable,—so manifest is the conclusion that it need scarce be mentioned.

A bad effect or none at all—such is the only alternative: if it could be proved to be innoxious, it would only be by being proved to be inoperative.

§ 9. *Mischief 5. Furnishing pretence for misrule by abuse of prerogative.*

If, to any persons who, with such a tale in their mouths, should presume to call themselves, as if for distinction sake, *King's friends*, any credit could be due, not merely the life of a single female, but the internal peace of a great nation, and with it lives, in numbers that defy all limits, have for years stood predestinated to eventual sacrifice by a sort of Jephthah's vow.

What does not belong to the present purpose is the pretencelessness of the application: what does belong to it is the principle: and such is the principle, that under and by virtue of it, with religion on his lips and wickedness in his heart, there exists not that system of tyranny and misrule, which a king might not find or make for himself an equally good warrant for the perpetuation of,—make for himself, by an apparent obligation, covering a real licence.

At the pleasure of the wearer, adamant or gossamer,—such are the chains imposed by that sort of law, of which the directive part being composed of vague generalities, the sanctionative part is composed of the ceremony of an oath.

1. That the course taken by government ought to be determined—not by the exigencies of the existing times,

but by the exigencies, to any degree different, of times to any degree remote—

2. That, in matters of law and government, men ought to hold themselves precluded from the use of reason, and from the benefit of experience—

3. That, for the governance of the *living* the proper heads and hands are—not those of the *living* but those of the *dead*—

4. That, by an idle and universally contemned ceremony, (for such it will be seen to be, as often as destitute of support from punishment it is seen to stand alone)—that, by a trick thus flimsy, it ought to be considered as being in the power of improbity or folly, in one disastrous moment, to preclude all imperfection from improvement, all injury from reparation—all abuse from correction—all mischief from remedy—all wickedness from repentance.

Opinions such as these, supposing it possible for them to be sincere—might surely of themselves, without any thing more insane, if any thing could be more insane, be considered as creating, on the ground of insanity, a necessity of taking the reins of government out of the hands of a monarch upon whom they could be proved.

Co-extensive with that portion, to which, in the field of administration and legislation, it applied by direct words, an opinion of this sort would, if delivered in the character of a deliberate and determined rule of action, be an act of *actual* abdication; and, in relation to the remaining part of the field, consideration had of its utter and irreconcileable incompatibility with good government, ought it not to be considered as having, by necessary inference, virtually the same effect?

Come when it will, is this of the number of those doctrines which are got up for the time?—No verily—but of those which apply to all times or to none.

§ 10. *Misrule, how to perpetuate—Coronation Oaths amended.*

In the character in which this instrument has so often been employed, viz. that of an instrument of perpetuation, applied to human ordinances, let but the use of it be admitted,—the instrument employed accordingly, and employed with the effect intended,—what shall it be said is the result? The result is—that in every shape, in which it can happen to the rulers of nations to have, or to suppose themselves to have, in any shape an interest in misrule, in misrule in any shape, perpetuity is secured to it.

As to the mode of operation nothing can be surer. To this or that word, of those which are in continual use, and which, without the aid of the instrument, are actually and habitually employed to this same purpose,—to any word of this sort—nor is there any scarcity of them—apply the instrument, the problem is accomplished—the thing is done.

Take for instance the word *innovation*. On whatsoever occasion they are for the first time respectively carried into effect or proposed, the best measures and the worst have this in common, that they are *new*. So long as any law or established practice in government exists, to which the appellation of *an abuse* can with propriety be applied, the removal of such abuse—in one word *reform*, viz. in relation to such abuse—must ever be among the measures, to which, if to any, the epithet of *good* belongs with indisputable propriety:—with a degree of propriety still more out of the reach of dispute than that of any measure, the object of which confines itself to *melioration* or *improvement*;—to the introducing in any shape a new and positive good, of the number of those without the aid of which the business of society has hitherto been conducted.

Under its own name, consistently with the established forms of decency, nor consequently with any satisfactory expectation of success, *abuse* cannot, in any shape, be by any person defended; as little can *reform*, at least in so far as it is understood to go no further than the removal of acknowledged abuse, be opposed. But *innovation*,—whatsoever may have been the import attached to the word,—not only *may* find, but continually does find, opponents:—and numerous and most strenuous opponents. *Innovation* is a term applicable to any thing whatsoever that is new: by it is denoted the introduction of any thing that is new: and, as every thing whatsoever, and therefore amongst other things, *reform*, in whatever shape, and to whatever subject and in whatever shape applied, is on its first being brought on the carpet *new*; therefore, so it is that whoever can succeed in getting condemnation passed on *innovation*, succeeds thereby in getting condemnation passed on reform: condemnation for everlasting, on reform to whatsoever *abuse* applied: in getting—if not perpetuation—actual perpetuation—at any rate judgement of perpetuation, passed in favour of abuse, in whatsoever shape it may then be, *or may thereafter come to be*, in existence *.

Add and say—*or may thereafter come to be*: for, erroneous, howsoever at first sight plausible, would be the supposition, that by the exclusion of new measures of government—by the exclusion of new laws—*abuses* would as well as new *reforms* be excluded. *Reform* cannot be effected without regulation,—*reform* cannot be effected but *by* regulation. *Abuse* needs no re-

* It has moreover the effect of conveying, in company with the idea of the principal object, as above, the collateral idea of the judgement of *disapprobation*, as passed upon such object by the person by whom it is employed. This being the case, in diminution of the mischief suppose it observed, that, on that consideration, it may be supposed to be meant to confine itself in its application, to the case in which the particular measure in question is of the number of those which, by that person, are or would be disapproved of. But, no assertion to this effect being directly and explicitly conveyed, no such obligation, as that of considering it as thus limited, is imposed upon him: and therefore, instead of being the worse, is but so much the better, adapted to the sinister purpose here in view.

gulation for the introduction of it. Not that it is, in its own nature, less capable of being introduced by regulation than reform is: but, forasmuch as things, which cannot be introduced but by regulation, cannot be introduced without being exposed to public observation, while things, that are capable of being introduced without regulation, are thereby, generally and comparatively speaking, capable of being introduced without being exposed to observation,—and since, for example, among the most frequently exemplified, as well as most pernicious shapes, in which abuse is apt to introduce itself, is that which consists in the habit of profitable and unpunished transgression in despite of regulation,—and, forasmuch as the evading of such regulations, by which sinister interest, in any shape, is opposed, is among the naturally constant objects of every individual, whose situation exposes him to the action of such sinister interest,—hence it is, that of any act of public authority, by which exclusion were put upon new measures in the lump, and without any particularized exception or distinction, the effect, in so far as it had any, would be to shut the door for ever against reform in every shape:—leaving it, to abuse in every shape, wide open,—with full liberty to receive increase—in every shape, and to any amount, and at all times.

The above observations premised, here then follows the recipe, for the explanation of which they have been premised:—a recipe or direction, for employing with precision and effect, on the occasion of the vast and complex ceremony termed *a coronation*, the simple ceremony of an oath, in the character of an instrument for the perpetuation of abuse.

Clause the third in the *Coronation Oath*. Stat. 1 W. and M. c. 16. § 3. "*Archbishop or Bishop*. Will you, "to the utmost of your power, maintain the laws of "God, the true profession of the Gospel, and the Pro-"testant Reformed Religion established by law? And "will you preserve unto the Bishops and Clergy of

" this Realm, and to the Churches committed to their " charge, all such Rights and Privileges as by law do *or* " *shall* appertain unto them, or any of them?"

Amendment proposed:—To the above words substitute or add the following, viz. *And will you to the utmost of your power resist all innovations in Religion and Government*, or *in Church and State?* " *King.* All this I promise to do . . . So help me God."

What is fortunate is—that in the above clause the anti-reformist possesses not only a most convenient *receptacle* already fitted up, but a *precedent* of the most sacred texture:—a precedent which, having its manifest origin in this very purpose, has already done whatsoever could then be done, towards the accomplishment of it.

A more ingenious or successful operation of ecclesiastical policy never was performed. Taking advantage of the fears of popish tyranny, excited, in every provident as well as in every protestant bosom, by the incidents of the day, here was an instrument made and provided for the nipping of reform in the bud, in whatsoever quarter in the field of established religion it should ever presume to show itself: an engine serving with equal effect for defending *Protestantism* against *Catholicism*, and *Church-of-Englandism* from reform and improvement, in every imaginable shape: preserving to the Right Reverend and Reverend persons therein mentioned the full benefit, not only of all such profitable abuses, if any, as they had already found means to introduce and establish, but of all such *others*, as by themselves or others, means should thereafter, and hereafter, be found for introducing and establishing, *for* or *to* their benefit, to the end of time.

Applied to government in its largest sense, established religion included,—among the characters of an instrument of perpetuation upon this model, is—that of being in a peculiar and extensive degree adapted to the purpose of giving perpetuity, or, if that be impossible, the utmost possible length of undue continuance, to *bad* systems in contradistinction to *good* ones: and the worse the system,—the greater is the need it has of this sort of instrument, the greater the service it is capable of receiving from it.

Applied in particular to religion established by law, it is in a like degree well adapted to the purpose of giving and securing the utmost possible degree of credence,—or, if not of *credence*, of silent *submission* and *acquiescence*,—to whatsoever is *false* in matters of religion, in contradistinction to whatsoever is *true*.

In the mouth of a *Mollah* or a *Bramin*, the first clause of it, ending with the word *God*, would with as much force and propriety, and without need of amendment, serve for the perpetuation of the religion of *Mahomet* or *Bramah*, as for any that calls or ever called itself the religion of *Jesus*—"Will you, to the utmost of your power, "maintain the laws of God?"

Applied to the tenets of any religion, or of any of the various editions of any religion, it includes in it moreover a certificate of the erroneousness and falsity of such tenets. Not that, by this or any other human contrivance, a religion that is true can *itself* be rendered false: not that by this or any other contrivance a set of facts, that have actually had place, can be made not to have had place. What it is *not*, is therefore a proof of the falsity of any religion to which it is applied: but what it *is*, is—a proof, nor needs there a more conclusive one, of a want of belief in affirmance of such religion, in the breast of those who concur in the application of it.

What?—if these notions or pretended notions of yours concerning your religion, be conformable to truth,—if it be the pleasure of the Almighty that the alleged facts on which it rests shall obtain credence,—is it not in the power of the Almighty, without your assistance, to obtain credence for it? You, whoever you are, is it that in yourself you have a power which has been denied to God? But for such assistance as it may please you to give, is the Almighty impotent?

With equal force and efficacy is it adapted (this same first clause) to the purpose of insuring submission to the most absurd conceptions, and to the most pernicious ordinances: to the most pernicious ordinances, and in their support, in case of need, to the most atrocious persecution and tyranny.

This or that ordinance which, by any portion of the King's subjects, is not regarded as of the number of the laws of God, suppose for example that by *the King* it is regarded, or pretended to be regarded, in that light? In the course of any exertion, made by him, in the endeavour to cause these refractory subjects to regard it in that same light, or at any rate to act and speak as if they did, suppose him to experience resistance: resistance, the effect of which, in whatsoever shape, more or less gentle or vigorous, it may happen to it to present itself, shall be to render it, in his judgement, impracticable to produce the effect he aims at. The clause continuing to be understood as it cannot but be understood, what is the practical consequence?—that, so long as the effect remains unproduced—no measure is there, be it ever so coercive, that he does not remain still under the obligation of bringing up to the charge. But the stores of his power are not, nor therefore is the virtue of his obligation, exhausted, till all the expedients that ever have been, all that ever can be, employed, by tyranny in all its shapes, by force and fraud combined, have been exhausted:—till, in his legislative character, he has refused his concurrence to all laws tending to the alleviation of the established yoke;—till in his *executive* or *administrative* character, including the virtual initiative part, which, by the hands of his servants, he bears in legislation, he has exhausted all the stores of corruptive influence in the endeavour to overpower and subdue all resistance, and given to the yoke every necessary and practicable increase of pressure.

To considerations of this nature a peculiar degree of importance is given, by the circumstances of the time*: when from such numerous, and in particular from such high-stationed mouths the cry is so loud for one knows not what succedaneous manifestations of hostility, under some such

* Written March 1812.

name as *pledges* or *securities*, or GUARDS:—as if there were any real *danger* but from such *guards*.

What?—More oaths?—more subscriptions?—more pretendedly perpetual laws?—and this for the security of the majority against the minority, of the wise against the foolish, of the strong against the weak?—Yes: when you have stocked both Houses with gunpowder, for security against fire.

What you *may* thus perpetuate is the remembrance of your own folly: what you *can* not and will not perpetuate, should men be weak enough to receive them, are —any such perpetually foolish laws.

§ 11. *Mischief* 6. *Corrupting the national morals and understanding—Oxford University Oaths.*

THIN are the partitions by which the moral and intellectual parts of man's frame are divided: scarcely can corruption gain the one without making its way to the other.

When, in the shape of an immense mass of unperformable engagements, all sanctioned by an oath, the seeds of perjury had been thus thickly sown, it could not be long ere they began yielding such their fruits: fruits more or less bitter to some stomachs, but at any rate conspicuous to all eyes:—a remedy was deemed necessary.

The simple course would have been to abolish the oath: but this would have been contrary to more than one fundamental principle of ecclesiastical polity.

1. One is—that the Church is infallible; that is, that a set of professors, who, at the expense of the people, are paid by the sovereign—such of them as do any thing—for reading and endeavouring to explain a most important indeed, but not the less obscure and mysterious book,—written at different times, before the use of printing, in different dead languages,—remain for ever, as they and their predecessors have been for two hundred and fifty

years past, under the happy incapacity of putting in any one instance a wrong sense upon it *.

The influence of this attribute displays itself in both departments of the mind; the understanding and the will: *opinions*, real or pretended, are by it converted,—that is, the words given as containing the expression of them are converted,—into *articles of faith: acts of the will*, of which, when issuing from the pen of acknowledged authority, the expressions become *laws*, are converted into—what certain laws of the Medes and Persians were once pretended to be—*everlasting* and *immutable* laws or ordinances.

Between the immutability that belongs to *articles of faith* and the immutability that belongs to *laws*,—between the essential characters of these two productions of the one attribute *infallibility*,—the nature of the *subject-matter* has however produced some difference:—*articles of faith* admit neither of *substraction* nor yet of *addition*; nor consequently of *change* or *substitution*, which is composed of *substraction* and *addition* put together: *ordinances* are equally unsusceptible of *substraction*,—but of *addition*, consideration had of the changes and chances to which the affairs of this transitory life are subject,—of *addition*, so it be made but rarely, nor then but with a sparing hand, they are not altogether unsusceptible.

To *herself*, Holy Mother Church—*Sancta-Mater Ecclesia*—younger and revolted sister of the church of Rome—reserved the superior establishment, the manufactory of articles of faith. It was set up and worked out,—the moulds accordingly all broken up,—the necessary assortment being

* Having operated as a stumbling block when employed by the Church of Rome, it seems to be understood, that in and by the Church of England the term *infallibility* shall not be employed. In practice however the thing itself, the attribute so denominated, is not the less assumed (it will be seen) and grounded upon: so that in the articles of liberty and security all that is gained to the people by the relinquishment of the term, is the substitution of a circumlocution to the proper appellative, while, by the *grammatical impropriety*, the *political*—the *despotic*—*pretension*, and its supporters, are screened in some measure from the reproach so justly due.

compleated, compleated for all eternity, so long ago as the year 1562.

To her two daughters—Kind Mother Oxford University, and Kind Mother Cambridge University,—*Alma Mater Academia Oxoniensis, Alma Mater Academia Cantabrigiensis*,—(for thus it is that, as often as they talk in Latin, the two goodly fellowships of Heads of Colleges, when acting in their legislative capacities, respectively style themselves,) she gave up the subordinate establishment—the manufacture of *ordinances*: ordinances, by which the minds of the flower of the English youth were and are to be moulded,—to the *form* at any rate, whatsoever may become of the *substance*,—of orthodox *piety*, of *virtue*, and of what little there may be, that is conducive to such orthodoxy, in *knowledge*.

The above, how pregnant soever in practical consequences, is itself no other than a theoretical principle: another,—itself a practical one, the practical object and fruit of the theoretical one,—is—that the minds of men are by these their rulers to be kept in a state of perpetual *dependence*: of dependence as abject and entire as possible.

Lest the conduct of these possessors of power should experience any inconvenient check in the opinions of the persons subject to it, matters were accordingly, and are to be, so ordered, that all notions of duty, moral as well as religious, religious as well as moral, are to be resolved into one much more simple obligation: the imagined *obligation*, produced by skilful culture out of the *liberty*, of submitting,—submitting on all occasions, and without reserve,—to the *opinion*, real or pretended, and thence to the *will* of these the ruling and domineering few. Such being the *end*, behold one necessary *means*.

When by the ruling powers such is the species of dominion aimed at, a necessary condition is,—and such accordingly is their interest,—that, on the part of the subject herd, transgression should be as universal and as continual as possible: that thus, finding in their own consciences nothing but condemnation, they should, with an intensity of self-assurance proportioned to the enormity and multiplicity of such their transgressions, behold, in the authority of these their spiritual guides, their only hope,—their only prospect of deliverance from the wrath to come.

In every community,—it is of the *obedience* of the men subject to authority that the *power* of the man possessed of authority is composed: in proportion to the need which each person so subject conceives himself to have of the beneficial exercise of such authority, will be the strictness of that obedience: proportioned to the self-attested wickedness of the sinner is the magnitude of the demand he has for absolution, in whatsoever shape and from whatsoever hand such deliverance may peradventure come.

Thus it is, that,—the effective power of the confessor being as the multitude and enormity of the sins, real or imagined, of the penitent,—it is in that respect the interest of the confessor, that, in the eyes of the penitent, and thence that in reality, these sins should be as multitudinous as possible: and thence for example it is, that, without exception or distinction, the words *miserable sinners*—*us miserable sinners*—are regularly crammed into their mouths: that so, by a perpetual fever, a perpetual demand for opiates, such as the laboratory of the confessor is furnished with, may be kept up.

Under the church of Rome the potion is administered in the *retail*, way,—drop by drop, *by hand* as it were,—to each patient by himself: and accordingly it is under that one of the two churches that the subjection is most entire: under the church of England, under the dominion of its universities, it can only be administered in the *wholesale* way: it can only be administered, as if it were *by steam*, to the whole flock of penitents in the lump. In this mode, to administer it with any chance of effect required no small degree of art: it has been, or will presently be seen, what that art has been, and with what success it has been practised.

To the accomplishment of the *design* thus indicated,

the course thus pointed to being, in the situation in question, if not the *only*, the most promising and directly leading course,—so, of the *existence* of such *design* the taking of that course, which has thus been seen to have been and to continue to be taken, cannot but be acknowledged to be *evidence:* evidence, the probative force of which is as the degree of pertinacity, wherewith a system necessitating a constant and universal habit of perjury—a system, having certainly for its effect the *generation* rather than the *prevention* of so many of the acts which itself prohibits,—a system for which, considered in these its peculiar features, no other assignable use or object can be found,—is upholden and persevered in: persevered in in sullen silence, without defence because without possibility of defence, in the midst of repeated and persevering remonstrance and reproach.

A self-styled *Explanation* of the oath,—bound up indeed in the same volume with the oath, but neither referred to by it, nor so much as, by the operation of the press, placed near to it,—such has been, and such continues to be, the instrument employed to *both* these purposes.

In pursuance of this design, a new principle in morals and legislation, and that a fundamental one, it was found necessary should be advanced: a principle, which, in itself, considered in an intellectual point of view, will be seen to be not less glaringly *absurd* than in effect as well as in design *pernicious:* advanced it required to be, and advanced it was and continues to be accordingly. By any being invested with authority, and acting in pursuance of that authority,—such an one excepted, if such an one there be, whose moral essence is composed of pure malevolence,—*punishment* (it seems now to be pretty generally understood, unless it be where the influence of such contrary doctrine as is about to be mentioned has been prevalent,) is never aimed at or regarded in the character of *an end:*—*prevention, viz.* of delinquency, being in every case the end,—punishment, *a means* directed to that end:—an instrument, how unwillingly soever, yet, under the spur of necessity, employed notwithstanding, in the character of *a means.*

According to this other,—this *anile*, for such it may be called, any thing rather than *maternal*, theory, which it was found necessary for Mother University to set up in opposition to the theory of common sense and common humanity,—according to this theory, punishment is not a *means* leading to prevention, but a co-ordinate *end* placed by the side of it on the same level: so that, when, by a person in authority,—say a parent, say a master, say a legislator,—any act is forbidden to be done,—a punishment being appointed to be inflicted in case of its being done,—in every such case, whether the *act* be *abstained from*, or the *punishment* be *inflicted*, is—in his eyes, and to his wishes—a matter of indifference.

In the world at large, in the case of murder for example, suppose a legislator taking up the pen and saying, "*Thou shalt not commit murder. Whoso committeth murder shall be hanged.*" To this legislator, according to the Oxford theory, it is matter of indifference how many murders are committed, so long as for every man murdered there is another man hanged.

Suppose in this case—(not that there could be any use in it)—suppose an oath taken by every man that he will never commit murder. By this oath, according to the same theory, would any man's conscience be bound to abstain from committing murder?—Not it indeed: all that it could be bound to would be,—in case of his committing murder and being unfortunate enough to be found out and prosecuted to conviction,—all that the man would stand thus engaged for, is—to stand still while the rope is putting about his neck.

As to the *subject* part of the community,—as it was in the beginning, so it is now,—it is in this *explanation*, including the theory on which it grounds itself, that such of them as feel any need of any such remedy find an opiate, such as it is,—and that the only one,—for whatsoever agitation their conscience may have been subjected to, by the consciousness of continually repeated perjury. As to the *rulers*, their well-seasoned consciences have needed neither *that* nor any other sedative. From one sin alone could they receive any sensible spasm;—and *that* is—the giving up the article of infallibility, nominal or real, as above mentioned. Sooner than give up *that*, they would all of them promise and vow to say the *Bismillah*,—as some of them, in the midst of their pious abhorrence of Popery, do still, it should seem*, to say *mass*. As to Laud's *Explanation*, if to them it were any thing, so far from an opiate it would be a caustic: for, by it are specially marked as perjuries those things, which (omissions included) they are, all of them, doing every day and all day long: under it they are, all of them, so many—(is it the fault of those who thus *act*, or of those who, that it may be no longer acted, thus *speak* of it?)—are, all of them, so many specially declared and posted *perjurors*†.

* Ex. gr. at Magdalen College; *viz*. by the Oath there taken for the observance of the College Statute. See in *Ayliffe's Hist*. i. 365 as *per Terræ Filius*, i. 15. Anno 1726; Dialogue between *Cartwright, Bishop of Chester* and *Hough, then President of the College*, and by *Terræ Filius*, stiled "*the present Bishop of Worcester*." Anno 1813, does this Oath, with the Statute in question unabrogated, continue to be administered. Like quære, in regard to the several other Colleges.

† Not to speak of the absurdity of this theory upon the face of it, it is not without full notice of the practical consequences of it, that these reverend guardians and instructors of youth have persevered so determinately in the propagation of it. To one of their own number—to that same Principal of Hertford Hall, afterwards Hertford College,—it had been an instrument of grievous annoyance. In despite of both sanctions, political and supernatural,—in despite of prohibition and oath together,—a scholar of his had *marooned*: in the 40*s*. penalty, under favour of the explanation of the oath, the fugitive, and the ruling member of a College that received and harboured him, had found, instead of what it professed to be, *a bar*, what it was in effect, *a licence*: and, at the price of these 40*s*., the act of migrating from one of those seats of piety and morality to another,—this act, which, supposing it an offence, is more than ten times as bad an one, (so, it will be seen, says the penalty) as that of being taken in the act of fornication without licence,—had received its expiation:—the faith of both sinners, in the power of they know not who, to absolve them from their oaths, having made them whole. Against an abuse thus dangerous to his authority, the reverend disciplinarian, in a lamentation of no fewer than 207 pages, gave vent to his complaints: but, though the root of the mischief lay in the first place in the *oath*, in the next place in the *explanation* by which that same oath is explained away,—so fundamental a doctrine is the doctrine of infallibility, and so incompatible with it

What is manifest all this while is—that, to the purpose of *prevention*,—which, except under such tutorage, is every where regarded as the sole object of every law considered in the character of a *prohibitive* one,—the effect of all this apparatus, binding and loosing together, is less than nothing. Without any such system of contradictions, the law of the land,—not quite so well obeyed, any more than quite so well in all points deserving to be obeyed, as could be wished,—does however, upon the whole, obtain a tolerably sufficient measure of obedience. But this theocratical code,—with its oath and its explanations, and its perjuries and its equivocations,—and under the name of principles of legislation its principles of misrule,—what, with all its ingenuity, and all its piety, has it done, but to expose itself to contempt, and its religion along with it?

Such would be its *inefficiency*, if prevention of mischief, its *pretended*, were its *real* object: but, its real objects being such as have been above explained, sure, too sure it is,—that, with relation to *those* objects, *inefficiency* cannot, with truth and justice, be imputed to it*.

would have been the abolition of abuse in any shape however flagrant;—that, although, in the abolition of one or other or both of these conflicting institutions, he could not but see his only remedy, yet—so perfectly hopeless was the prospect—that the dose of courage, necessary to enable a man to come forward with a proposal for the application of this only remedy, could never, in all these 207 pages, nor at any time afterwards, be mustered up.

* Besides scattered articles in other places, in *Tit. xv. de moribus conformandis*, to look no further, among the contents of pages from 173 to 179, section from 2 to 8, inclusive, are found regulations in abundance, from the violation of which no man who ever passed so much as a week—not to say a day—in the University, unless it were in a state of confinement, can, it may safely be said, have been exempt—not to go further back—for these last fifty years.

No. 1. p. 173. § 2. *Offence* prohibited—Walking about *at leisure* (or else *in an idle manner* according to the construction which the interpreter finds himself disposed to put upon the word *otiosi*) in the city or its suburbs.

Penalty—For the first offence, in the case of an undergraduate, reproof or chastisement at the discretion of the Vice-Chancellor or of the Proctors: in the case of a graduate, fine of two shillings to the use of the University.

Justification or *exemption*—Reasonable cause, to be approved as

§ 12. *Mischief* 6. *continued.*—II. *Cambridge Oaths.*

SUCH, in regard to *oaths* and *perjury*, being the state of things in *one* of the two chief sources and seats of Church-of-England piety, what is it in the *other?*

such by the Proctors or the Vice-Chancellor. What is meant for the *time*, at which, to produce the effect of justification, the approbation is to have been bestowed,—viz. before the act, or after it,—*i. e.* whether an *ex post-facto* allowance will suffice, or a previous and express licence is necessary to have been obtained,—these are among the doubts to which no solution is afforded, either on this case, or in any of the following ones, in some of which it may be found perhaps not altogether so obvious as in *this* it seems to be.

" Statutum est (says the text, § 2.) quòd Scholares (præsertim " juniores et non graduati) per civitatem, ejusve suburbia, *otiosi* non " obambulent; neque in plateis . . . . aut apud oppidanorum seu " artificum officinas, stantes aut commorantes . . . . conspiciantur.

" Si quis absque rationabili causâ, à Procuratoribus vel Vice-Can- " cellario approbandâ, hâc in parte delinquens deprehensus fuerit, si " non graduatus fuerit, pro arbitrio Vice-Cancellarii vel Procurato- " rum corripiatur, vel castigetur. Si graduatus fuerit, 2*s*. Univer- " sitati mulctetur."

No. 2. § 2. *Offence* prohibited—Being *seen* in the streets, standing or staying at the shops or workshops of town's-people. *Penalty* and *justification*, as in No. 1.

After an excursion made to the Sessions and the Assizes, for the purpose of keeping out the sanctified youth from those seats and sources of profane law, as below, the statute returns to the subject, and declares once more, that scholars and graduates of all sorts shall abstain from the *houses* (such is the word now) and shops of the town's-people:—viz. in the *day-time*, and now it is added at *night*—*Penalty* and *justification*, or *exemption*—what will be seen, when that very miscellaneous section, with the rest of its contents, comes under review.—Statutum est, quòd scholares et graduati cujuscunque generis, à *domibus* et *officinis* oppidanorum, de *die*, et presertim de *nocte*, abstineant.

From 1759 to 1768 certainly, to 1794 probably, in the occupation of the townspeople, amongst shops of other descriptions, were, and it is supposed, to this day are, coffee-houses, fruit-shops, not to speak of *Inns* and other specially prohibited places, of which further on, and moreover booksellers shops:—the booksellers shops, it is supposed, not wholly unfrequented; the others thronged.

No. 3. § 3. p. 174. § 3. *Offence* prohibited—Being present at the *Sessions* or *Assizes*.

Penalty—For the first offence, 10*s*. without distinction of grade or condition: in case of order, by the Vice-Chancellor or the Proctors, to depart, and non-compliance therewith, imprisonment: of

The answer is,—to the purpose of *sincerity*, widely different: but, as will presently be seen, to the purpose

the oath taken, as above, special commemoration made, and also application of it to the purpose of securing—what?—not immediate compliance, viz. departure from the seat of judicature, but the eventual departure to the seat of imprisonment. The offence having, at the time of the enactment or confirmation of this statute, viz. about the year 1634, been, it seems, a very alarming one, the expression *then* given to the alarm has continued to be repeated ever since.

Justification or *exemption*—Reasonable cause, "to be approved by "the Vice-Chancellor:"—no other approbation sufficient.

"Statutum est," (says the text, § 3.) quòd nullus scholaris cujuscunque conditionis ad publicos et generales conventus juridicos, vel civitatis vel comitatûs Oxon. (qui *Sessiones* aut *Assisæ* vocantur) nisi ex causâ rationabili, per Vice-Cancellarium approbandâ, accedat, vel iisdem interesse præsumat, sub pœnâ 10*s*., unicuique ibidem deprehenso infligendâ; et incarcerationis, etiam omnibus et singulis per Vice-Cancellarium vel Procuratores inde recedere jussis, nec obtemperantibus; cui adeundi carceris mandato, (quia grassanti incommodo alias commode occurri non potest) omnes et singuli virtute juramenti Universitati præstiti, obedire teneantur.

"Juniores autem, Tyrones, et alii non graduati (qui illuc spectatum maxime confluere solent) ibidem deprehensi pro arbitrio Vice-Cancellarii aut Procuratorum, pœnas dare teneantur."

No. 4. p. 174. § 4. *Offence* prohibited—Being *caught* (for to *fornication* applies, it seems, in this code, the principle which in that of Sparta is said to have been applied in case of *theft*,) being caught in the day-time in a house in which prostitutes are kept. (Quere if but one prostitute?) "*Præcipuè* verò, ab ædibus infames seu suspectas mulieres vel meretrices alentibus, aut recipientibus . . . . . abstineant."

Penalty—In the case of an under-graduate, arbitrary; at the discretion of the Vice-Chancellor or the Proctors, by whom the catch has been made: in the case of a graduate, 3*s*. 4*d*. Price 3*s*. 4*d*. a time, *pro quâlibet vice*, as often as he pleases.

Justification or *exemption*—Reasonable cause of entrance or continuance (nisi rationabilem accessûs sui moræve causam reddiderint).

No. 5. p. 17. § 4. *Offence* prohibited—Being *caught*, as above, with a prostitute in any private chambers:—*in privatis cameris*: viz. in a man's own chambers, or those of any other gownsman.

Penalty and *justification* or *exemption*, as above.

For so natural an amusement, 3*s*. 4*d*. may to some eyes appear rather a high price for a licence: but, when it is considered that it must be a young man's own fault if ever he is called upon to pay it, (and then there is the bawdy-house-keeper to pay in one case, and the girl to pay in every case) it will scarcely, upon due consideration, be pronounced excessive. If prevention were an object, the act really meant to be prevented would, it should seem, here be—not, of the main position, viz. that of the *impropriety of the ceremony*, much the same.

as might at first view be supposed, *fornication*, but *stinginess* or *negligence:* in either case, the not giving a bed-maker's boy 6*d*. to keep watch: or in the case of the bawdy-house, choosing one that has not a back-door to it.

"§ 4. *De domibus oppidanorum non frequentandis* statutum est, quòd scholares et graduati cujuscunque generis, à *domibus* et *officinis* oppidanorum, de die et præsertìm de nocte, abstineant. *Præcipuè* vero, ab ædibus infames seu suspectas mulieres vel meretrices alentibus, aut recipientibus; quarum consortio scholaribus quibuscunque, sive in *privatis cameris*, sive in ædibus *oppidanorum*, prorsus interdictum est. Et si quis de die in eisdem vel earum aliquâ *deprehensus* fuerit (nisi rationabilem accessûs sui moræve causam reddiderit) si non graduatus sit, pro arbitrio Vice-Cancellarii, vel Procuratorum qui deprehenderunt, castigetur. Si vero graduatus fuerit, 3*s*. 4*d*. pro quâlibet vice Universitati mulctetur."

No. 6. p. 175. § 5. *Offence* prohibited—Being in any *inn*, *cook's-shop*, *tavern* or other *house*, in which wine or any *other drink*, or tobacco are ordinarily sold: unless for a necessary and urgent cause, to be approved by the Vice-Chancellor or the Proctors. The offence being in this case so much more serious, the punishment is accordingly so much more severe, than for fornication, or for negligence betrayed in either of the modes above mentioned:—for an undergraduate under the age of 18, *a public whipping:* for one above that age, or a graduate, 6*s*. 8*d*. with a string of ulterior punishments in case of relapse.

"Statutum est quod scholares cujuscunque conditionis a diversoriis, cauponis, œnopoliis, ac domibus quibuscunque intra civitatem vel præcinctum Universitatis, in quibus vinum, aut quivis alius potus, aut herba nicotiana sive Tobacco ordinarie venditur, abstineant, nisi ex causâ necessariâ et urgenti, per Vice-Cancellarium aut Procuratores approbandâ.—Quodque si quis secus fuerit, octodecim annis minor, nec graduatus, *publicè castigetur:* major autem annis octodecim, pro primâ et secundâ vice sex solidis et octo denariis Universitati mulctetur."

Booksellers'-shops, if there be any such places there, are in the houses of towns'-people: and so are *coffee-houses:*—if the justification allowed in the case of *bawdy-houses* had been extended to these other lounging-places, would the indulgence have been excessive? Not that any such notion is meant here to be insinuated, as that going to a bawdy-house is as bad as going to a bookseller's-shop:—this is not the mark aimed at. All that is meant is—that, as in the case of the bawdy-house a reasonable cause, approved as such by his reverend superiors, saves a young man harmless, so might it even in the case of the bookseller's-shop. Homicide has its *justifications:* and why not the going into a shop? even though it be a bookseller's:—and so in the case of coffee-houses.

No. 7. p. 173. § 7. *Offence* prohibited—Being *found* out of one's

At Cambridge, on admission into the state and condition of a member of the University, an oath, to the same effect as above, together with other effects in abundance,

College in the evening, after the Christ Church nine o'clock bell has tolled, viz. in any house or street within the precincts of the University.—*Penalty*, in the case of an under-graduate, arbitrary: in case of a graduate, 40*s.*: with eventual imprisonment as for a breach of the peace.—*Justification* or exemption, showing a reasonable cause, to be approved as such by the Vice-Chancellor *and* the Proctors.

Under this code, the penalty for being caught in the *street* being 40*s.*, while the penalty for being caught in a *bawdy-house* is but 3*s.* 4*d.*, every prudent young man, who, while he is in the street at a forbidden hour, spies a Proctor who he suspects spies *him*, will, if there happens to be a bawdy-house within reach, run into it—were it only for refuge: and this, judging of offences by punishments, being of the two so much the less serious, can not but, as such, obtain at least a comparative approbation, on the part of these reverend disciplinarians. Unfortunately, whatever was the intention, the words are here so extremely general,—"*domo quâcunque—every house* "*whatsoever*,"—that, if caught, a man would be no better off in the bawdy-house (supposing it to have struck nine) than, in the street. But, if the house has a back-door to it, as every bawdy-house ought to have, he will *not* be caught, and then every thing will be as it should be.

.... "Omnes scholares cujuscunque conditionis .... ante nonam "horam (quæ pulsatione .... &c. denuntiari solet) ad collegia et "aulas proprias se recipiant .... Quodque si quis postea extra colle- "gium proprium vel aulam, in *domo quâcunque* vel *plateâ*, vel alibi "intra præcinctum Universitatis *repertus* fuerit (nisi causam rationa- "bilem ostenderit per Vice-Cancellarium et Procuratores approban- "dam) si non graduatus fuerit, pro arbitrio Vice-Cancellarii vel "Procuratorum puniatur, vel castigetur pœnâ corporali, si per ætatem "congruit, alioqui quadraginta solidis mulctetur: quas mulctas a "quibuscunque deprehensis exigere, et ipsarum semissem in Fiscum "Universitatis redigere, tenentur Procuratores fide suâ datâ Univer- "sitati."

No. 8. p. 174. § 8. *Offence* prohibited—1. Playing at any game at which people play for money; for example dice and cards:—or with balls, in the courts or gardens of the town's people. *Penalty*, in case of an under-graduate, of a fit age for being flogged, flogging accordingly: in case of a graduate or an under-graduate above that age, 6*s.* 8*d.* *Justification* or *exemption*, none.

Statutum est quod scholares, cujuscunque conditionis, abstineant ab omni lusûs genere in quo de pecuniâ concertatur; veluti a lusu talorum, alearum, et chartarum pictarum, necnon a lusu globorum, in privatis oppidanorum areis hortisque; nec hujusmodi publicis lusibus per Statuta Regni prohibitis, intersint; quodque nemo intra Univeris exacted. But, subjoined to the formulary, and on the same paper, is printed *an explanation*, by which, one point excepted, and that an useless one, it is declared to amount to nothing. The engagement thus sanctioned is—what? an engagement to pay *obedience* to these same statutes, all or any of them?—No: but only,—in case of disobedience, and prosecution and conviction and judgement accordingly, and execution denounced,—an engagement to *submit* to it, and in so doing to be *humble**. "*Excerpta è Statutis Acad. Cantabrigiensis, &c.* Cambridge. J. Archdeacon. 1785."

On this occasion surely, if on any, is one of Moses's

sitatem hujusmodi ludis se exercentes excipiat: sub pœna castigationis corporalis non graduatis (quibus per ætatem congruit,) aliis vero et graduatis, 6*s*. et 8*d*.

No. 9. ib. 2. *Offence* prohibited—Sportsmanship in all its branches. Of the *genus* of offence, the description is—every kind of play or exercise by which to other persons danger, injury, or inconvenience is produced: *species* exemplified, amongst others, hunting wild beasts (such as deer, hares, and rabbits): among *things*, mentioned as being in this account to be abstained from, are—dogs, ferrets, nets and snares, guns, cross-bows, and hawks.

Item, quod abstineant ab omni genere lusûs vel exercitii, ex quo aliis periculum, injuria, vel incommodum creatur; veluti a venatione ferarum (ut damarum, leporum, et cuniculorum) cum canibus cujuscunque generis, viverris, retibus, aut plagis; necnon ab omni apparatu et gestatione bombardarum, et arcubalistarum; sive etiam accipitrum usu ad aucupium; sub pœnâ castigationis corporalis, &c. ... præter suspendium canum, et forisfacturam .... retium &c.

Unless in the interval of about forty-four years the state of things in this seat of learning, morality, and piety has undergone in the above respects a total change, very little less than the *quicquid agunt homines*, not only in Laud's time was, but to this day remains, involved in this catalogue of transgressions.

* Memorandum. August 3, 1804. Found the printed copy from which what follows is printed,—found it, together with several other copies—on the pavement of the Senate House at Cambridge, and by leave of the person who shewed the house, and in presence of three other persons, took it away with me. J. B.

Juramentum à singulis Scholaribus in Matriculatione suâ præstandum.

Cancellario Procancellarioque Academiæ Cantabrigiensis quatenus jus fasque est, et pro ordine in quo fuerim, quam diu in hac republicâ degam, comitèr obtemperabo; Leges, Statuta, Mores approbatos, et Privilegia Cantabrigiensis Academiæ (quantum in me est) observabo; Pietatis et bonarum literarum progressum, et hujus commandments broken, and the Lord's name taken in vain,—if by *taking in vain* be meant *taken to some bad purposes*, and to no good ones: yet *so* taken in vain, as that, upon the so taking it, no such thing ever takes place as perjury.

Comparing together the state of opinions and religious feelings in these two seats and sources of Church-of-England piety, a few results,—in an historical point of view at least, not altogether devoid of interest,—present themselves.

1. That, at *Cambridge* as well as at *Oxford*, there was a time at which *perjury* was not regarded as a matter of complete indifference.

2. That at *Cambridge* as well as *Oxford* some person or persons was or were found, in whom symptoms of a desire to be exempted from it had manifested themselves.

3. That, by the ruling powers, at *Cambridge* as well as at *Oxford*, in compliance with such desire, measures were taken for the relief of those consciences, in which, on the score in question, symptoms of uneasiness had thus broken out.

4. That, in this view, neither at *Cambridge* any more than at *Oxford*, did it please these reverend potentates to pursue the simple and only proper course, *viz.* as above, to divest of this extraordinary sanction the comparatively trifling regulations in question, leaving them to the sup-

Academiæ Statum, Honorem, Dignitatem, tuebor quoad vivam, meoque suffragio atque consilio rogatus et non rogatus defendam: Ita me Deus adjuvet, et Sancta Dei Evangelia.

3. Jul. 1647.

Placet vobis, ut in majorem in posterum cautelam jurantium et levamen, hæc verba sint annexa Juramentis Academiæ Matriculationis, Admissionis, Creationis;

"Senatus Cantabrigiensis decrevit et declaravit eos omnes qui monitionibus, correctionibus, mulctis, et pœnis Statutorum, Legum, Decretorum, Ordinationum, Injunctionum, et laudabilium Consuetudinum hujus Academiæ transgressoribus quovis modo incumbentibus *humiliter* se *submiserint*, nec esse nec habendos esse perjurii reos."

Et ut hæc vestra concessio pro Statuto habeatur, et infra decem dies in libris Procuratorum inscribatur.

port afforded by those ordinary sanctions, to which the general law of the land, and with it not only the *well-being* but the very *being* of society, is confided.

5. That, at *Cambridge* as well as *Oxford*, the influence of the principle,—above spoken of as being common to the ruling powers, under every modification of the *Christian* religion (not to speak of *others*) when by law *established, viz.*—the assumption of infallibility,—openly announced, or necessarily howsoever covertly implied,—is on this occasion discernible. To the standard of opinion and conduct, matter may, in case of urgent necessity, be *added*, but from it none is ever to be *taken away*.

6. That, for the purpose in question, at *Cambridge* the course taken was such, that thereafter whatsoever other objections it may remain open to, as above, still in that seat and source of piety, on the score of a violation of the sort of *oath of obedience* in question, no person, living in a state of perjury, has perhaps ever been, or was likely to be, found:—while, in *Oxford*, what seems highly probable, not to say certain, is—that, bating rare and casual exceptions,—as in the case of confinement by sickness,—from that time to the present, no member of the university, by whom the oath, which is administered to all above the age of childhood, has ever been taken, has ever dwelt in that seat and source of piety for two days together, without living in the habitual commission of that sin.

7. That the form of *government* under which, at *Oxford*, perjury was thus rendered universal and perpetual,—to this time, and by the blessing of God to all future time,—was *monarchical: viz.* during the vigorous part of the joint reign of *Charles I.* and *Archbishop Laud*:—the form of government, under which, at *Cambridge*, it was abolished as above, was *republican: viz.* that of the *Long Parliament*.

8. That the *religion* under which perjury was thus *established*, was the religion, which, in England, having along with the monarchy been restored, remains still established, was *episcopalian—Church-of-Englandism*:—the religion under which at Cambridge perjury was *abrogated*,

as above, was *Presbyterianism:* viz. under the same Long Parliament.

Without incurring the reproach of misrepresentation, the distinction thus brought to view could not have been passed over without notice.

Not that, to the present, or to any other practical purpose, the importance of it presents itself as very considerable. In both seats of piety, so perfectly and universally does it appear to be understood, that, applied to the purpose in question at least, an oath is a mere *matter of form*, i. e. that it amounts to nothing, and is of no use,—and that, where it is not punishable, *perjury* is a sort of a thing that no man need put himself to the trouble of being ashamed of; that no instance, it is believed, was ever known, in which, in the circumstance of being exempted from this perjury, a member of the University of Cambridge has been heard or seen, *in public* or *in print* at least, to speak of himself as possessing any advantage.

True it is—that, in both seats of well-paid piety, a man hears indeed, now and then, as of other good things, so of a good thing called by the name of *Christian liberty:* but, under this appellation, whatever else be the meaning of it, no such liberty as the *liberty of not perjuring one's self* appears, in either of them, (with the exceptions above brought to view in the case of Oxford,) to have been considered as comprised.

Of a yoke, which sits so light upon the shoulders by which it is borne, it is not natural, that, by the mere force of sympathy, the pressure should be rendered very grievous to others, to which it does not extend itself.

On any such ground between the children of the one sister and those of the other, have any symptoms either of sympathy, or of heart-burning, ever presented themselves?—No, never.—If, on the shoulder of the Oxonian, a piece of a feather having been deposited by the wind, it happened to the man of Cambridge to observe it there, what he might or might not do, is—the picking it off,—what it is certain he would not seriously do, is the taking the relief so administered for the subject-matter of boast, or the burthen for the subject-matter either of reproach or commiseration. Instead of the *feather* on the *shoulder*, suppose the consciousness of *perjury* in the *bosom*, the result will be the same.

Piety is one thing: sincerity is another. In both seats of every thing that is right and proper, in all proper places, on all proper occasions, piety continues to be professed: of sincerity,—at least in so far as concerns an aversion to perjury, or to falsehood in a declaration of opinion concerning religion,—in a case where any thing is to be got by it, no such aversion seems ever to have been manifested, except by here and there a scabby sheep or two, who for that cause have, upon occasion, been cast out of the flock, being not without reason regarded as not well assorted to the company into which they had been introduced.

In the House of Lords, the bench of Bishops,—in some proportion at least—but which, unless it be to a father who has a son to prepare for the reception of the Holy Ghost, seems not to call for any very anxious inquiry,—is divided between the Right Reverend persons whose piety has had the milk of the *one Alma Mater*, and those in whose breasts the same useful quality has had the milk of the *other kind mother*, for its source. On any of those occasions on which the influence exercised by a speech is understood to depend in so great a degree upon the personal reputation of the speaker, was any Cambridge-bred ever heard to claim, at the expense of any Oxford-bred prelate, any superiority in the scale of trustworthiness?—A stare, as if Lord Stanhope had just spoken, is the only reply which a question to any such effect could reasonably expect to receive.

The conclusion is—that, in both of the two original *sources* of that piety, the profession of which is so well paid for with public money, as well as in that elevated *reservoir* which has its place in the House of Lords, an oath is universally considered as *mere form*; and that the breach of it, when not understood to expose a man to visible punishment,—the breach of it, termed in one word *perjury*, is regarded as a matter of indifference;—a sort of act of which no man need be ashamed.

The result here spoken of in the character of a mischief being the corruption infused into the system of public morals, and it being among the positions here maintained, that an oath is a ceremony devoid of use, the contempt thus shown to be entertained for it cannot (it may perhaps be said) consistently with this position be placed upon the list of mischiefs. True: in so far as the contempt is confined to the ceremony,—to the ceremony considered by itself. But in that ceremony is included an assertion, and by the falsity of that assertion *sincerity* is violated: in the perjury, a sort of insincerity is included: and, for and by every grain of insincerity which enters into the composition of it, every human character is by so much the worse.

As matters stand at present, while, in the character of a security for sincerity, or for good conduct in any other shape, the nothingness of the ceremony is as yet unacknowledged,—while, on the contrary, you will see it so frequently spoken of as the very basis on which society rests, and without which the whole fabrick would fall to pieces,—so it is that, by what is regarded as a profanation of the ceremony, and a violation of the obligation supposed to be contracted by it,—contracted by its own single virtue,—indication is given of a *looseness of principle*, as the phrase is, or, in a language somewhat more determinate, of a comparative insensibility to the transgression-preventing influence of the three tutelary sanctions, as hath been elsewhere indicated and explained *.

All this while, to bear a man out in the breach thus made in what is universally, and without any contradiction, spoken of in the character of a most sacred duty, to protect him against reproach—nothing whatever is there but *custom*.—Custom? and of what sort? a custom of acting—not in conformity, but in opposition, to the

* Introd. to Rationale of Evidence, ch. 7. § 7.

dictates of honest judgement: a custom analogous to a custom of smuggling, or a custom of false coining: a custom of doing that which he, whose custom it is, believes to be wrong, and feels himself unable to find any thing to say in justification of.

It imports—(this habit of perjury)—it is produced by, and itself goes on producing and fortifying, the *custom* of regarding the distinctions between right and wrong as depending upon *custom* and nothing else. If the difference between *happiness* and *unhappiness* depended upon custom, so would that between *right* and *wrong*. Unfortunately this is not the case. By the custom which men of one colour have so long been in of seizing men of another colour when they could get at them, and keeping them in a state of slavery, what is easy enough to see is, how the sufferings of the men thus dealt with are created, what is not easy to see is, how they are lessened. By the custom which men with one set of religious phrases in their mouths have so long been in, of keeping in a state of humiliation and hopeless degradation men with another set of religious phrases in their mouths, what is easy to see is, how, in the minds of men thus dealt with, irritation is *created*: what is not easy to see is, how it is assuaged.

Not that, either under monarchy or under episcopacy, perjury has ever *eo nomine* been put upon the list of essentials, and the obligation of committing it considered as constituting the matter of a 40th article. At the utmost, the *breaking* of oaths can but be considered as of the number of those exercises which are left unprohibited, in such sort as to be "*when the magistrate requireth*" lawful, just as by article the 39th the *taking* of them is.

To an eye which should confine its view to the state of things as in this respect it exists at Oxford, it might be apt to appear, that, in the eyes of those fathers of the church whose seat is in the High Place, the propagation of perjury has been and continues to be an object of importance. Turn however to Cambridge, and you will see immediately either that with the Right Reverend persons in question this has not been at all an object, or that, if it has, the benefit that would result from it has been considered as outweighed by some inconvenience that would result from the putting of the business at Oxford upon the footing on which it stands at Cambridge: for example, a shake given to so pious and useful a doctrine as the doctrine of *virtual infallibility*, as above*.

Things being as they are, that, with the Right Reverend persons in question, the propagation of the practice in question either has never been at all an object, or at least has never been an object of preponderant importance, is demonstrated by experience. For, if it had been, matters would, before now, have in such sort ordered themselves, that the Oxford instrument intituled *Explanatio Juramenti* would at Cambridge have been substituted to the decree without a title, by which the Oxford perjuries have been prevented from establishing themselves at Cambridge:—and thus that *uniformity*,

* Add to this, in the instance of those whose piety has for its source the sincere milk sucked from the breast of *Alma Mater Oxonia*, the indecorum which would attach upon any such humiliation, as that of receiving a sort of correction at the hands of her *younger sister*.

Figure of rhetoric all this, it is true: but, where *Church* is concerned, argument is never carried on with any other instruments. In every question concerning the doctrine or discipline of an established Church, there are certain *postulates* which must be assumed and admitted in the character of *first principles*: principles such, that he who should presume to include them in the subject matter of inquiry, would be a man not to be argued with:—that a certain number of men, mostly old or middle-aged, or an uncertain portion of that number, compose together at pleasure, at one time, one preeminently beautiful, howsoever antient, as well as pious and in every respect excellent and admirable, woman; who has a family of her own, composed of fathers and sisters and daughters, and whatsoever else is necessary:—at another time a most spatious, lofty, magnificent, antient, and venerable building:—at another, a collection of admirable rules and ordinances:—at another time, all human beings whatsoever, who either believe, or are supposed to believe to be true, what this beautiful woman, *i. e.* these old and middle-aged men, say is true, or who are forced to pay them for saying so.

which on other occasions has been so dear to *the church*, (*i. e.* to governing men) and for which *the church* has (*i. e.* men governed by them have) been made to pay so dearly, would there also, and on this occasion, have been established.

At present, in this as in so many other instances, the object of importance is—that oaths should be taken: for the accomplishment of it, effectual provision continues accordingly to be made. The question of no importance continues to be—whether, after having been taken, they have been kept or broken: and for this they have accordingly been left to take their chance.

After all, this practice of taking oaths, whatsoever may happen to them when taken, to what is it that in these latter days it is indebted for its continuance? Answer—Not so much to its *absolute* and intrinsic, as to its *relative* importance; relation being had to the grand object of objects—*jargonicè, the peace of the Church:* in plain language, the preserving from disturbance the ease of so many high seated persons, spiritual and temporal, sacred and profane: a blessing which cannot but be subjected to more or less disturbance, as often as the eye of scrutiny is directed to a subject so little able to abide it *.

So again, on the other hand, in the case of the mischievous applications made of it, for example, on the occasion of the recent associations among the malefactors called *Luddites*. What can *not* be proved is, that in any one of the instances, in which, to the mischievous purpose in question, an oath has been administered by

* Inoperative to beneficial purposes, operative to mischievous ones,—inoperative to the purpose of securing testimonial verity for the use of justice, operative to the purpose of securing fidelity to mischievous engagements,—positions thus contrary, how (it may be asked) can they be reconcileable?

The answer is—that when, with a view to practice, spoken of in the character of a security for testimonial verity and pronounced inoperative, *that* which, to the making good the position, is not, in that view, necessary, is—that the ceremony should not, in any individual instance, have operated in the direction and with more or less of the effect in that case intended: what is sufficient is—that them to one another, it has actually, by its separate influence, been productive of any binding, of any mischievous fidelity-securing, effect: for, independently of any such superstitious tie, other forces acting in that same direction are but too plainly perceptible, *viz.* in case of fidelity the prospect of success, in respect of the accomplishment of the mischievous object, whatever it be, which, by the supposition, is a common one; in the case of defection, the fear of vengeance at the hands of the associates who would thus be deserted and betrayed.

But, at the same time, what *is* proved, is—that, in the opinion of the persons by whom the oath is administered, it *does* promise to operate with the desired effect, upon the persons to whom it is administered: and, in their situation, being by the tie of common interest, and with the advantage of opportunity, engaged, each of them, to form the truest judgement concerning the texture of each other's minds, and this for the express purpose of determining what sort of force is likely to operate upon them with the greatest effect, thus it is, that, for regarding the instrument in question as likely to operate to the mischievous purpose here in question, the public has the best evidence that the nature of the case admits of.

On the subject of *university oaths*, another observation, that may perhaps present itself in the character of an objection, to the conclusion inferring the inefficiency of the ceremony as a security for testimonial verity, from

whatsoever beneficial effect it may, in this character, have been productive of, over and above what might without any inconvenience have been produced without its assistance, would not have been considerable enough to compensate for the evil, produced in various shapes, by the various mischievous applications made of it, as above.

In particular instances individually taken, whether it has or has not had any and what separate operation, is a matter of fact wholly out of the reach of ascertainment.—Why?—Because this never is applied, but in conjunction with these other forces, *viz.* that of near-impending punishment and that of present shame. The consequence is—that, in these same instances, as it cannot be proved to have had *any* operation, so neither can it be proved to have had *none*.

its inefficiency in the character of a security of habitual obedience to the regulations thus sanctioned, may be thus expressed. Conclusive as is the proof given of the inefficiency of this ceremony to that purpose, in that seat of distinguished piety, among that class of pious men, what does not follow, is—that on the occasion of judicial testimony, even supposing the profane checks to mendacity altogether removed, this religious ceremony would, even in the instance of the same persons, be completely inoperative.—Why?—because the *oath against disobedience* is administered once for all: *viz.* on entrance, and not afterwards: whereupon, human weakness considered, nothing is more natural, than that, of the impression made by the ceremony, the force, howsoever great at the moment, should in general act more and more faintly at every successive point of time, till sooner or later its action came to be equal to 0.

But, in the case of the *judicial oath*, the time, at which the act which it is employed to influence comes to be performed, follows instantaneously upon the ceremony: instantaneously, and before the impression made by it, whatever it may be, has had time to lose any of its force.

That the observation has a degree of truth in it, can scarcely be denied.

But, on the other hand, as in the case of the statutes in question, occasions for the fulfilment, and thereby for the breach of it, are occurring every day,—under these circumstances, suppose the engagement to be renewed every day, the ceremony to be repeated every day,—exists there in this case any sufficient reason for supposing that, from such an arrangement, the degree of observance would, in the whole body taken together, receive any considerable increase?—Not it indeed.—A discovery would soon be made,—and as soon, very generally, not to say universally, received,—that the ceremony was *a matter of form*—*a mere matter of form*. And, be it *oath*, be it *subscription*, be it what it will,—no sooner is it understood that the operation is a matter of *form*, than its efficiency, if it ever had any, is at an end. He who, speaking of an engagement of any kind, terms it *a matter of form*, says in other words,—"I do not hold myself bound by it."

In the case of an instrument derived from a supernatural and extraordinary source,—such as is the fear of expected future—but never in this life experienced or observed—punishment,—the impression made by it seems likely to depend for its force in no inconsiderable degree on the *unfrequency* of the application made of it: in the case of an instrument, derived from a natural and ordinary source,—such as is the fear of visible and frequently observed, if not also experienced, punishment,—the force of the impression does not seem, in an equal, if in any degree, liable to abate.

§ 13. *Practice of receiving judicial oaths, its repugnancy to the precepts of Jesus.*

How palpably repugnant to the precepts of Jesus many of the observances are, to which men are compelled, under the notion of their being enjoined by the religion of Jesus, is what could not easily be conceived by any, who, on such occasions, are not in the habit of using their eyes, nor will be believed by many of those who are.

"Again," (says the account in Matthew, v. 33, the only one of his four biographers by whom any account is given of this precept) "Again, ye have heard that it "hath been said of old time, Thou shalt not forswear "thyself, but shalt perform unto the Lord thine oaths: "(33.) But I say unto you, Swear not at all: neither "by heaven, for &c (35.) Nor by the earth, for ... &c. "neither by Jerusalem: for ... &c. (36.) Neither ... "by thy head, because ... &c. (37.) But let your "communication be Yea, yea; Nay, nay: for whatso-"ever is more than these cometh of evil."

As to what is to be understood to have been here meant by "*old time*," the only passages of the Mosaic law, as reported in the Old Testament, that have any bearing upon the subject, (at least as far as the marginal references can be depended upon) are those which are in Exodus (xx. 7.), Leviticus (xix. 12.), Deuteronomy (v. 11).

In *Exodus* (xx. 7.) the words are these, "Thou shalt "not take the name of the Lord in vain: for the Lord "will not hold him guiltless that taketh his name in "vain." These are the words, in the authentic translation of that portion of the Jewish Statute Law, which, in the Church of England Liturgy and other offices, is distinguished by the name of *the ten commandments*, of which it stands third.

Next comes *Leviticus* (xix.) in which the words are these (11.) "Ye shall not steal, neither *deal falsely*, "neither *lie* one to another. (12.) And ye shall not "*swear by my name falsely*, neither shalt thou *profane* "the name of thy God: I am the Lord."

Lastly comes *Deuteronomy* (v. 11.) in which the words are exactly the same as in Exodus.

Will it be said, that by the words "but shalt *per*-"*form* unto the Lord thine oaths," it appears that the sort of oath meant by Jesus to be forbidden was the promissory oath alone, and not the assertory oath?

But 1. In the promissory oath the assertory oath, it has been seen, is included.

2. And, in the above passage in Leviticus, the *assertory*, in which is included the *testimonial* oath, is specially mentioned. "Ye shall not lie one to another—Ye "shall not swear by my name falsely, neither shalt thou "profane the name of the Lord.—Ye shall not swear "by my name *falsely*"—says the law of Moses. What says the law of Jesus? Ye shall not swear *falsely?*—No:—but *Swear not at all*. "Ye shall not swear *at all*." In this prohibition the words are general, all comprehensive. If, in respect of judicial occasions or any other occasions, it had been his intention that any exception should be made, would not such intention have been *expressed?*—would not this have been the *occasion* for ex-

pressing it? If, of words thus plain and positive, the only obvious import is not to be trusted to, would it not be better that, instead of being in such multitudes distributed, all Testaments, old and new, should be burnt, and the Church of England Common Prayer-book, with its articles of faith, and other appendages, distributed instead of them? *

3. And accordingly comes the concluding passage of the words of Jesus, in which the word, employed in contradistinction to *swearing*, is "*communication.*" Under this word *communication*, is not *assertion—statement—narrative*,—which soever be the name given to that application of the faculty of discourse which is most in use;—is it not still more obviously and necessarily included, than any such comparatively rare application as is made by what is called *promise*, *engagement*, deliberate and solemn *engagement*?

The words of James—will *they* be acknowledged as the words of Jesus, or as conformable to and explanatory of the meaning of the words of Jesus?—"But "above all things, my brethren," says that Apostle, (v. 12.) "swear not: neither by heaven, neither by the "earth, neither by any other oath: but let your yea "be yea, and your nay, nay, lest ye fall into condem-"nation."

* True it is, that, in the same chapter (v. 17.) "Think not" (says Jesus) "that I am come to destroy the law or the prophets: "I am not come to destroy, but to fulfill .... &c." But, from this passage, can the oath-and-perjury compelling powers think to extract a warrant for the exaction or reception of the *assertory*—the *judicial* oath?—Can any such notion be maintainable, as that—the assertory, the testimonial, the judicial oath having been allowed by the Mosaic law—the prohibition of it by Jesus would *pro tanto* be a *destruction* of that law, and therefore, consistently with the explanation thus given by him, cannot be supposed to have been intended?

In the first place,—although true it is that, if the ordinance in question were of the *positive* cast, *commanding* the thing in question to be done, a posterior law, *prohibiting* that same thing from being done, would *pro tanto* be destructive of such prior law,—yet, whereas, in the present case, that which by the posterior law in question is *prohibited*, was by the prior law not *commanded* but

On either of these occasions respectively, did Jesus—did James—explain, and say—"on a *judicial* occasion, or "for a *judicial* purpose, swear as much as you will, for in "such case swearing is not swearing?"—On the day when this letter was written by James, had such been the meaning of his master, was it not high time for the disciple to have made known as much?

On this ground stands the system, by which, on pretence of Christianity, Christians in such multitudes, together with all such other persons, to whom it may happen to stand in need of their testimony, are thrust out of the protection of the law:—of that branch of it, viz. the *penal*, on which alone men are altogether dependent for whatsoever protection is afforded to them against the most grievous of the injuries to which man's nature is exposed.

All this while,—without any the smallest innovation upon Church-of-Englandism—upon that system in comparison of which all perceptible happiness and unhappiness is as dust upon the balance—without any such horrible and impracticable temerity, (will men believe as much when they see it with their own eyes?)—the practice of administering oaths might be abolished. No:—not indeed, if so it were, that, by any one of the thirty-nine Articles, the practice is enjoined: but on the contrary so it is, that, by the only article which has any application to the subject, what is declared is—not the

only *left unprohibited*,—what is *not* true is—that, without special words in the prior law to guard against such prohibition, any such *destruction* would, in common understanding, be understood to be effected.

In the next place, if, by the prohibition of the *assertory* oath or vow, the Mosaic law would have been destroyed, then so was it by the prohibition of the *promissory* oath or vow:—for, that this was in contemplation, and by Jesus meant, if any thing was meant, to be included in the prohibition, is put out of doubt by the word "*performance*"—"but shalt perform unto the Lord thine oaths." By these are plainly meant oaths capable of being *performed*, i. e. *vows*: promises—intelligible and serious promises—capable of being performed; not that species of nonsense, which, under the name of *profane* swearing, stands prohibited under 1*s*. and 5*s*. penalties by English Statute law.

obligatoriness—but merely the *lawfulness* of employing this instrument.—The lawfulness? Yes.—Lawful then let it be:—at any rate, so as the *practice* of employing it be done away, the *doctrine* concerning its lawfulness, taking the word *lawfulness* in a religious sense, may without much mischief remain unquestioned and undisturbed.

If so it really were, that in all testimonial cases the employment of this supposed security were obligatory, what should be said of those, by whom, to so great an extent as has been seen, it has been left unemployed?

Obligatory or unobligatory, useful or unuseful, the practice at present maintained in relation to it will in either case be indefensible.

§ 14. *Succedanea—True securities substitutible to this false one.*

MENDACITY is an instrument applicable to the purpose of every wrong. Punished in any one instance, why should it be left unpunished in any other? Punished, in the character of an instrument of delinquency employed in the commission, perpetrated or attempted, of an offence,—in what *proportion* should it be punished but according to the nature of the offence?

Should the prevention of wrongs—should the prevention of offences—be purposely left to accident? Then to the prevention of wrongs, in the commission of which *mendacity* has been or would be employed as an instrument, the application of punishment should be purposely left, as at present, to accident.

Mendacity is not an uniform offence: it changes its colour according to the nature and substance of the offence to which it is rendered or endeavoured to be rendered subservient. *Mendacity*, employed in drawing down upon an innocent head the destroying sword of justice, is *murder:* murder, encompassed with all its correspondent terror. *Mendacity*, employed in the obtainment of money, is but *depredation*. Yet, while *predatory* mendacity is punished with death, the punishment for the *murderous* mendacity is in comparison but a flea-bite*.

The principle being admitted, the application presents no difficulty. By apt description, performed in and by one all-comprehensive rule or short series of rules, the punishment destined for mendacity might, without difficulty, be attached to it, in every case in which testimony comes to be received for any legal purpose:—in every case, those included, in which, under the existing system, it would be thought fit to employ, for the purpose, the ceremony of an oath.

For any *warning*, that might be thought requisite to be given,—given, viz. by the denunciation of the eventual punishment, as at present by the ceremony,—for any such warning, *magistracy—public functionary*—there needs none. With or without reference to those denunciations, of which so strong and ample a provision is to be found in the sacred books,—a *formulary* being provided by the legislator, for pointing out the punishment to the notice of the person in whose testimony he had an interest, any the humblest individual would not be less competent than the highest-seated magistrate.

Judicature, grounded on testimony, delivered before mutually chosen arbitrators, sitting in the seat of *natural* procedure, *might* in this case, and, if not purposely debarred from it, *would*—receive that adoption, which at present is *in effect* refused to it, granted but *in pretence*.

For the eventual punishment to attach,—and, for that purpose, to distinguish legal investigation from simple conversation,—a short formulary might be *pre-appointed*.

Not that at present, under the existing system, any such

* When will the language of truth be the language of law and office? When mendacity is punished by the House of Commons, it is punished as a *contempt*: never as any thing but a contempt: always as a contempt:—when, so frequently, not *contempt* but *fear* is the cause by which it is known to have been produced.

tutelary caution is provided. For mendacity employed to no worse purpose than fraudulent and unterrific depredation, mendacity is in various cases, and without any such *warning*, punished with death: witness *personation;* witness, in an infinitely diversified set of instances, *forgery*.

In the state of things thus ventured to be proposed, another amendment much wanted might be made with as little difficulty. Falsehood, though not accompanied with that *evil consciousness* which in common speech gives it the epithet of *wilful*,—which in one word gives it the name of *mendacity*, and, if preceded by the ceremony, the name of perjury,—might, if accompanied with *blame* in another shape—in a shape, in which, in the language of the Roman school, *blame*, on the occasion of whatsoever mode of delinquency imputable, receives, and not unaptly, the name of *temerity*,—might be substituted to *punishment*, according to the *degree* of blame.

At present, under the system of oaths and perjuries, misstatement, from whatsoever *cause*—misstatement, in what *degree* soever mischievous and blameable—is either perjury or nothing. What is the consequence? That, where it *has not* been accompanied with that *evil consciousness*, but *has* been accompanied with *temerity*—with that heat and passion by which adequate reflection has been excluded,—it is either, under the name of *perjury*, punished on a false ground and to excess, or—what is more common and not less pernicious—left unpunished at least, if not successful and triumphant.

§ 15. *Cause and origin of the practice in regard to oaths.*

Thus repugnant to one of the plainest precepts of Jesus,—to that one which may perhaps be stated as being the most pointed and specific of all the precepts of Jesus,—how happens it, it may be asked, that, under a religion calling itself the religion of Jesus, the use made of this ceremony should have been so abundant?

After what has been said, the answer to this question will surely not be thought to lie very deep.

In the case of this as of other institutions, the final cause must be to be looked for, in the particular interests, of those by whom they were set on foot.

In so far as, on the occasion of the application made of it, the institution happened to be favourable to the general interest of the community, in so far the operation and effect of it was beneficial :—in so far as—the particular interest being repugnant to the general interest—the general interest was sacrificed to it, the operation and effect of the institution was pernicious.

What has had place in the instance of other institutions, may perhaps have had place in this ;—*viz.* that at their origin the balance of their effect has been on the side opposite to that on which it has come to be afterwards : at its origin,—being employed—though in itself an evil—as an instrument, and perhaps a necessary one, to the combating of still greater evils,—it may have been productive of a quantity of good, which, upon the cessation of these greater evils, has come to cease.

On the occasion of the question concerning the *effects*, good and bad, of the use made of this instrument, there are two distinguishable *states*, in which society requires to be considered : *viz.* a barbarous state, and a comparatively civilized state. In the barbarous state, that is until a certain degree of civilization has taken place, it may probably be impossible to determine, to any tolerable degree of certainty, whether the *good* or the *evil* were predominant : the chances may perhaps be found even in favour of the *good* :—while, in the civilized state, the good effects being altogether or nearly evanescent, the evil will, as above, be found *preponderant* in the balance, if not *alone*.

In the early and barbarous state of the species, anterior consequently to the days of history, take any number of human beings, connected by no other ties than those of vicinity,—could they or could they not have been knit together in the bonds of political society, and thence gifted with a till then unexperienced degree of security, without the aid of this or other kindred instruments?—If not, the preponderance on the side of utility seems to be out of the reach of dispute.

Among the ancient Greeks, great and various was the use made of oaths: among the Athenians more regard was supposed to be paid to them than in other parts of Greece. By Theseus the scattered population of Attica was, for the first time, brought to that degree of union, and into those habits of submission, by which political power and regular government are composed. In the production of this effect, the instrument in question would naturally be employed. Could the effect have been at all, or equally well, produced without it?

In the hands of the *priest*, supernatural hopes and fears have sometimes been employed, on the formation of society, in bridling and leading the passions of the multitude, sometimes, in a society already formed under the *military leader*, in the bridling of *his* despotism.

Suppose a case, in which, by the direction given to the *force* of the community, the peace and welfare of the community would but for some such principle of restraint be destroyed,—in such case, let any such principle present itself and come into action, here,—although the nature of it be such as to rank it under the denomination of *fraud, deceit, imposture*,—the preservation of the community may, in this restraining principle, how sinister soever in its nature, find its cause.

Suppose an infant in the cradle,—and a madman, with a sword in his hand, about to destroy it: if, by any representation, though it be false, the hand of the madman can be staid,—as for instance, that an angel with a flaming sword is about to smite the madman,—here the mischief, which in ill-directed *force* would have found its efficient *cause*, finds in *fraud* its *preventive*.

Next to the evils of anarchy, are the evils of despotism. Political society once formed, despotism is the predominant disease, to the attacks of which it remains continually exposed. Despotism or misrule has place, in so far as the force of the whole is, for the benefit of *the one* or *the few*, employed in a manner mischievous to *the many*.

If *fraud* could never be employed but to the promotion of *happiness*, fraud would not be *vice* but *virtue*.

In its own nature, fraud is equally capable of being employed on the side of force—of despotic force,—as an instrument in the hands of force,—or on a side opposed to it. Employed by force, or on the same side, it is an instrument of evil. But if so employed,—employed in such direction and manner, as to oppose, with more or less effect, the mischief that would otherwise be done by force, —in a word, to serve as a check to mis-applied force,—in this way it may be an instrument of good.

In the society in question, in the hands in question, the effect of *military* force unchecked would be (let it be supposed) a barbarous tyranny and lawless despotism. In such a state of things, imposture and superstition—on the part of a priesthood imposture, on the part of the people that superstition on which imposture must always depend for its success—may, if evils, be necessary evils: necessary evils, and, with reference to the disease, remedies; with reference to the impending calamity, blessings.

Take the case of Jephthah.—In the sacred history the collection of facts actually reported is not ample enough for the present purpose. But, for the purpose of argument, they afford a ground, ample enough to serve as a basis, upon which, for the purpose of argument, suppositions may be applied.

The facts are—that, being commander in chief of the army of the Jews who were at war with the Ammonites, he vowed a vow—that, in case of his coming off victorious, he would, in the way of sacrifice, put to death the first living object, that should present itself to him on his first visit to his own home. That first object was his only daughter, and accordingly put to death she was*.

* To certain divines this anecdote has not been an acceptable one: the sort of ingenuity, which has applied itself to so many

Let this then be the supposition. Jephthah was the military leader: in that quality his power was exercised in a manner dangerous to public liberty. In the influence of the priesthood he beheld a rival power: in that power his own power felt a check, and that a salutary one. The form and ceremony of an oath had all along been an instrument in their hands: on the observation he had made of the efficiency of it on other occasions, was grounded the application he thought fit to make of it in this. In the utterance given to this his oath, what he had in view thus eventually to deal with, was neither more nor less than the first that should happen to present itself, of the animals ordinarily employed on the occasion of sacrifice: for, though in the practice of employing human creatures on this occasion for victims, there was not to the people over whom he presided any thing new or even very strange,—and though their common ancestor Isaac would by his father have been thus dealt with, and the whole race thus extinguished; yet so it was, that no such thing was in his thoughts: least of all had he any such intention as that of all human beings his own daughter, his only child, should be thus dealt with. Unfortunately for the father and the daughter, such was the looseness of the expression, employed, or at least said to have been employed by him, in the utterance of the *oath* or *vow*, that human beings were not excluded by it.

When the time came for fulfilment, his endeavours were of course applied to the causing that sense to be put upon the oath, by which the dictates of humanity would have been conformed to, and his own affliction spared. But, in an incident thus tragical and impressive, the priesthood beheld an opportunity too favourable to be suffered

other reported facts and doctrines, has accordingly applied itself to this incident: endeavours have been employed to explain it away. But if in this part the sacred volume is not clear enough to be depended upon, neither can it be in any other: instead of a guidance, the whole of it is but a snare. He "*did with her according to his* "*vow:*" viz. "*offer*" her "*up for a burnt-offering.*"

to pass unimproved: an opportunity of giving the utmost possible degree of force and efficiency, to an instrument the management of which was in their hands.

The power thus possessed by them, and employed, was it, or was it not, with reference to the aggregate interest of the community in question—the Jewish nation at the time in question—a beneficial one?

For a categorical answer to this question no sufficient data are to be found.

Of a hypothetical answer the difficulty is not equally great.

The time was a time of war—a time, during which, the earlier and less experienced the state of society is, the less distinctly does the authority of a commander in chief differ from a despotism. In this state of things, the authority of Jephthah, did it stand in need of a check?—The sort of check, which the priesthood were able and disposed to apply, was it upon the whole a salutary one?—Both questions determined in the affirmative, the price paid for the keeping of this check in order and repair—that price, great as it was, was not perhaps too great. One individual—the father—afflicted: another individual—the daughter—sent out of the reach of affliction;—what are these evils, in comparison of those of a course of unbridled, and tyrannically exercised despotism, or of civil war, its desperate and perhaps still more afflictive remedy?

Thus much for Jephthah, and for the application made of the ceremony in his case. Upon the whole, whatsoever it might have been in times thus remote and different from the present, for a long time past its effects may surely, without any considerable error, be set down as altogether on the side of evil.

To the purpose of being employed as a security against transgression in any shape, and in the shape of mendacity in particular, it is—for so it has above been shown to be—altogether needless.

Its effects then are purely on the side of evil. Of evil it is, as hath been already seen, an instrument, in a variety of ways: and it is,—if not in a direct way in the evil of which it has been productive, at least in an indirect way in the good which the ruling few have contrived to extract out of that evil,—that the use made of this instrument has found its efficient or final cause, and the upholders and employers of it their motive for thus upholding and employing it.

In many cases, in the supposition of the event is involved that of the antecedence of its opposite. Relaxation supposes restriction: condescension supposes pride.

Prohibition forms the necessary antecedent to and ground of *licence:* and, when to profitable prohibition profitable licence is added, the produce of misrule is doubled.

There are two modes of culture in which the produce of licence may be reaped:—the *general* and the *particular*—the *wholesale* and the *retail* mode.

As to the *wholesale* mode, in its application to *mendacity*, its variations have been already shown, *viz. omission* and *explanation:* forbearing to apply the security to this or that class of cases, and explaining it away when applied.

The *special* or *particular* mode consists in the granting of *special licences* under the name of *dispensations:*—granting them avowedly, not covertly and indirectly as in those other cases.

The use derived, in this shape, from the system of oaths and mendacity-licences or perfidy-licences, by the Church of Rome, especially in times antecedent to that successful revolt against its authority which has obtained the name of *the Reformation*, is sufficiently notorious. By the ceremony of an oath, obligation applicable to any purpose was created: by a dispensation granted by the Head of the Church, an obligation thus contracted was, for the benefit of any person to whom on any terms it pleased the Holy Father to concede the indulgence, done away.

It was on the occasion of the *dispensation* more particularly, that the power of the spiritual ruler was most immediately profitable and most conspicuous. In the creation of the *obligation*, the tying of the knot was the operation of a prearranged *machinery*: the part taken in the operation by the Manager consisted in nothing more than watching over it, keeping it in order, and keeping it clear of obstructions.

The *dissolution* of the obligation—*the dispensation*—was a work that could not be performed but as it were *by hand*: on no occasion could it be performed, unless on that same occasion, if not the *mind*, the *hand* at least of the Manager were employed in the execution of it—in the production of the effect.

At the time of the Reformation, when men's eyes had begun to open themselves, this power of dispensation became too flagrantly mischievous to be retained by any priesthood that had revolted from that of Rome. The days were now over, when by *the power of the keys* treaties might be made and dissolved; kingdoms given and taken back; war kindled, and peace sold.

By the Church of England priesthood it was accordingly, with whatsoever reluctance, along with so many other of the powers of the Romish priesthood, given up. By Laud, as the crown by Cromwell, the cardinal's hat was refused. The power of *dispensation in the gross*—the power of *explanation* was all that was by *Laud's* power retained: retained accordingly it was, and in what manner retained and employed has been seen above.

In time past, and thence in time present—the cause, *final* or *efficient*, of whatsoever is at any time found established,—be it beneficial, be it pernicious, to the *subject many*,—will always be to be found in the particular interest, real or supposed, of the *ruling few*.

Of the institution here in question, at the time of its creation, the effects may—upon the balance, as hath been seen—have been either good or bad,—it is scarce possible to say which. But, those times having been long since passed, the question *now* is—not whether it shall be *set on foot*, but whether it shall be *preserved*: the use *now* made of it—the support *still* given to it—these are the subjects which call for consideration in this our time.

APPENDIX.

I. *Among the rulers of the University of Oxford, perjury universal and constant, as declared in and by an Explanation, given by themselves, in their own Statutes—its Jesuitical stile.*

In page 54, in speaking of the rulers of the University of Oxford, mention being made of a document, in and by which the guilt of perjury is in an especial manner declared to attach, upon every person who shall comport himself in the manner therein described;—the same being a manner, in which to his own knowledge and in the sight of the whole population of that city and its University, every such person does continually comport himself;—an extract is thereupon announced, as intended to be here subjoined, for the purpose of bringing to view the contents of that document, in so far as material to the present purpose. In the original, the following are the terms of it: annext to it is a translation, in the penning of which, *polish* being considered as *falsification*, the most scrupulous fidelity has been observed. Misrepresentation *pro tanto* would have been the result, if, any where, in place of that which *is*, any thing, of which it were supposed that *it might better have been*, had been substituted.—N.B. Of this document a copy is contained in every edition of that extract from the body of the University Statutes which is put into the hands of every member at his entrance.

ΕΠΙΝΟΜΙΣ,

Seu Explanatio Juramenti quod de observandis Statutis Universitatis a singulis præstari solet: quatenus, scilicet, seu quousque obligare jurantes censendum est.

APPENDIX TO THE LAWS,

Or Explanation of the Oath, which concerning the observance of the University Statutes is by each person wont to be taken: how far, to wit, or to what extent it is to be regarded as obligatory on the swearers.

Quoniam aliis restrictior et morosior, aliis contra, laxior et discinctior est *Conscientia;* illi levissimos quosque lapsus suos calumniari nati sunt, et sese non sæpius immorigeros, quam perjuros esse arbitrantur; hi quoscunque legum nexus, *jurisjurandi religionem*, conscientiæ laqueos, strophis suis eludere satagunt: et ipsi sibi palpum obtrudunt: non abs re fore visum est explicare, quatenus seu quousque *jurisjurandi, de Statutis Universitatis* observandis præstiti, religione teneri seu obligari singulos censendum sit; in eoque tale temperamentum sequi, ne, vel durius interpretando, illis crucem figere; vel benignius, his fibulam laxare videamur.

Forasmuch as in some men *Conscience* is more strict and morose, in others more lax and loosely-girded; the former are born to calumniate every the slightest of their own transgressions, and regard themselves as not more unfrequently unobsequious than perjured; the latter strive by their quibbles to elude all legal ties whatsoever, the religion of an oath, the nets of conscience, and themselves put a cheat upon themselves: it seemed to be not beside the purpose to explain to what length or how far each person ought to be considered as holden or bound by the religion of the *oath*, taken, touching the observance of the *Statutes of the University;* and therein to follow such a temperament, that, neither by too hardly interpreting it, we may appear to fasten a cross upon the one; nor by too benignly, to unbutton a button for the other.

Qua in re, hoc imprimis attendendum est; verbis statutorum, in quæ jurijurando quis adigitur, sensum genuinum, ut et obligationi sive vinculo *juramenti* modum ac mensu-

Wherein this is in the first place to be attended to; that by the words of those Statutes, in which any one is made to take an oath, the genuine sense, as also the mode ram præstitui seu prescribi a mente et intentione, non præstantis, sed exigentis juramentum; scilicet ipsius *Legislatoris*. Neque enim si quis inter jurandum, verbis, in quæ jurejurando adigitur, sensum affingat alienum ab eo quem *Legislatori* propositum fuisse, ipsi juranti persuasum aliasve verisimile est, (hoc est, hujusmodi sensum qui desidiæ vel socordiæ faveant, quive *disciplinæ Academicæ* aut morum honestati repugnet) eo ipso ευορκειν illum, aut statutis vel jurisjurandi religioni satisfacere putandum est, nedum jurisjurandi religione exolutum ut putet se quis, si ad jurandum animum afferat, non obligandi seipsum, sed in nudo verborum cortice sistendi: neque *poeticum* illud δυσορκιας remedium seu verius colludium—*Lingua juravi, mentem injuratam gero*,—homini Christiano satisfacere aut potest, aut debet, eo ipso a perjurii crimine excusatum reputare se ut debeat. Quoniam igitur mensura obligationis, seu vinculi juramenti, ab *intentione Legislatoris* præcipue pendet, operæ pretium utique fuerit, singulos mentem ac intentionem *Legislatoris* perspectam et exploratam habere; qualis scilicet qualiumque statutorum transgressio juratos ad omnia statuta promiscuè observanda perjurio involvat.

and measure of and to the obligation or tie of the *oath* is applied or prescribed by the mind and intention, not of him by whom the oath is taken, but of him by whom it is exacted; to wit of the *Legislator* himself. For neither if any one in swearing, affixeth to the words in which he is made to swear, a sense foreign to that of which he the swearer is persuaded, or on other grounds it is probable that it was that which was intended by the legislator (that is to say such a sense as is favourable to indolence or indifference, or repugnant to academic discipline or moral rectitude) is it to be thought that he swears rightly, or satisfies the statutes or the religion of an oath, nor yet let any one think himself released from the religious obligation of an oath, if to the act of swearing he brings the intention, not of binding himself, but of stopping at the bare bark of the words: for that *poetic* remedy, or rather shuffle-board to wrong-swearing—*Sworn is my tongue, but unsworn is my mind*—neither can nor ought to satisfy a Christian man, in such sort that he ought to repute himself thereby excused from the crime of perjury. Forasmuch therefore as the measure of the obligation, or tie of an oath, depends chiefly on the intention of the *Legislator*, it would verily be worth the labour that all persons should have held the mind and intention of the *Legislator* well seen through and explored; to wit of what sort, and of what sort of statutes, the transgression involves in perjury those who are sworn to the promiscuous observance of all the Statutes.

Intenditur igitur perjurio se obligare,

Primò, delinquentes....&c.
Secundò delinquentes....&c.
Tertiò, qui....&c.

Quoad alia vero delicta; si Statutorum pœnarumve *contemptus*, & crassa obstinataque negligentia abfuerit, delinquentes, si pœnis per Statuta sancitis, aliùsve arbitrariis se submiserint, *Jurisjurandi religionem* temerasse minimè censendi sunt. *Magistratibus* denique, prout major eis debetur reverentia, quàm ut pœnis passim intentatis coerceri ipsos et in ordinem cogi par sit, ita major *conscientiæ obligatio* incumbit; utpote qui non solum ea quæ sui muneris sunt fideliter *administrare*; verùm etiam, ut alii omnes suis officiis fungantur, sedulò curare tenentur. Neque tamen eos ubicunque officiis suis defuerint, perjurii protenus se obligare intenditur. Verùm quoniam *ipsorum fidei* Statutorum custodia et tutela concredita est, si (quod absit) per negligentiam aut socordiam suam Statuta quæcunque inusu ac desuetudine exolescere, et tacite

Accordingly what is understood is—that those men bind themselves in perjury,

First, who....&c.
Secondly, who ...&c.
Thirdly, who....&c.

But as to other transgressions; if *contempt* of Statutes and punishments, and gross and obstinate negligence are out of the case, delinquents, if they shall have submitted themselves to the punishments appointed by the Statutes, or otherwise to such as are arbitrary, are by no means to be deemed to have violated the *religion of an oath*. Lastly, on *Magistrates*, according as to them greater reverence is due, than that it should be right that they should be coerced and kept in order by such punishments as are all along threatened; so is a greater obligation of conscience incumbent; to wit as being they who are bound not only faithfully to *administer* those things which belong to their functions; but also diligently to take care that all others do perform their respective duties. Nor yet is it understood, that they, as often as they shall quasi abrogari patiantur, ipsos etiam fidei violatæ ac *perjurii* teneri decernimus.

have been wanting to their duties, do altogether bind themselves in perjury. But forasmuch as *to their fidelity* is intrusted the keeping and guardianship of the Statutes, if (far be it from them!) they suffer through their own negligence or indifference any Statutes whatsoever to be rendered obsolete by non-use or desuetude, and tacitly as it were to be abrogated, them also do we declare to be bound in the bonds of violated faith and *perjury*.

These "*Magistratus*"—these perjurers in grain—these *ipso facto* convicted and thus placarded perjurers,—who are they?—The Reverend the *Vice-Chancellor*—the Reverend the *Heads of Houses*—the Reverend and non-Reverend, but for the most part Reverend, *Masters of Arts* and other the graduates of higher degrees, being members of the House of *Congregation* and of the House of *Convocation* respectively:—for of these is the *Legislative* body composed. The Reverend the *Vice-Chancellor*—the Reverend the *Proctors* and *Pro-Proctors*, all for the time being—yea, and within the precincts, logical and geographical, of their respective jurisdictions, the Reverend the *Heads of Houses*, with their respective local subordinates:—for of these is the *Executive* body composed.

Quære as to the Noble the *Chancellor*, and the Noble the *High Steward?* Upon their respective *Installations*, or whatsoever else be the term,—by them respectively is not some such oath taken?—for are not they too "*Magistratus?*"

On the occasion of the Catholic question, an apprehension, lest, in the breasts of some, or many, or all of the religionists of that persuasion, the ceremony of an oath should not always operate with sufficient power—lest in the person of the Pope, notwithstanding their protestations to the contrary, they should upon occasion seek and find a power, willing, and in their opinion able, to exempt them from the obligation of it;—an apprehension to some such effect was, on the part of many if not all these reverend persons, among the reasons assigned for the wish to see, now and for ever, or thereabouts, still withholden, from between a fourth and a fifth part of the population of the two Islands, the common rights of subjects. The obligation of an oath to be done away at pleasure by an old priest, in or out of prison, upon the continent! as if in the bosom of every one of these reverend persons, by whom the sincere milk of the word has been sucked from the breast of Holy Mother, there sat not, in the character of a perpetual Pope, with a *sponge* in his hand, the image of Archbishop and University-Legislator *Laud*, constantly sitting and constantly at work, watching each perjury as it peeped out, and passing over it, in the manner that has been seen, the sponge of *dispensation*, the instant it came to view.

II. *The manufacture of perjury persevered in, and the produce repeatedly augmented,—with open eyes, and in spite of remonstrances.*

In pages 52 and 54, the determination to persevere in a course of universal and continual perjury, and the habit of enduring the reproach of it without flinching, rather than acknowledge on the part of this eldest daughter of Holy Mother Church the possibility of error, are mentioned as among the *arcana imperii*, inviolably observed in and by that closest of aristocracies—the government of the University of Oxford. If of so undeniable a proposition any further proof be requisite, it may be viewed in abundance in the course pursued by that government in the field of legislation for these last fifty or sixty years. Revision, not unfrequent:—revision of this very title, samples of which have here been brought to view:—Revision, but with what effect? with what view? Never with any such effect or view as that of taking any thing from the number of their perjuries; not unfrequently with the *effect* at least of adding to it.

At the time of *matriculation*—such is the technical term by which admission into the body of the University is there designated—under the title of *Parecbolæ sive Excerpta è Corpore Statutorum Universitatis Oxoniensis, In usum Juventutis Academicæ*, an Abstract of the University Statutes, containing such of them as it is thought fit that a person who is not a member of the governing body should be acquainted with, is put into his hands. It forms a well-filled 12mo volume: containing in the edition of 1756, 254; in the edition of 1794, (put into my hands within this seven months as the latest edition,) 261 pages.

In Title XV. *de moribus conformandis*, (being the title from which extracts are here given, as above) in the edition of 1756 the number of sections is 14, in the edition of 1794, 16.

Whence comes this variance?—The case is this: Between the date of the former edition and that of the latter, two Statutes—of the number of those which it was thought fit to make known to the individuals whose conduct was to be governed, and whose fate was to be determined by them—two universally promulgated, besides seven or eight secret or partially promulgated statutes, of which presently—had been passed.

In the edition of 1794, between § 5. *De oenopoliis* &c. and § 6. *De nocturnâ vagatione reprimendâ*, is accordingly inserted a section intituled *De vehiculis* (a section against *Phaëtons*) which, being § 6., changes the number of that which follows next to it, viz. that *De nocturnâ vagatione reprimendâ*, and makes it, instead of § 6, as in the above-mentioned earlier edition, § 7.

Lastly, at the end of this same *title* is moreover inserted an additional *section*, intituled *De reprimendis sumptibus non Academicis*, and which accordingly is numbered § 16, as will be seen presently: the day on which it passed is 16 Dec. 1785.

In the manual in question, viz. in the edition of 1794,

of neither of these additions is any intimation given; neither by mention made of their respective dates, nor otherwise.

But in this same interval, at various times, 9 or 10 in the whole, the body of the Statutes had been taken in hand for the purpose of *amendment;* each time in the form of simple *addition:* in no one instance in the form of simple *repeal:* and, since the date (1794) of the above-mentioned latest edition, reckoning to the present time (March 1813) it has undergone amendment in *four* other instances, of which presently.

Of the interpolated section *De Vehiculis*, I have not been able to learn the precise date. In the series of statutes at large, the date of the earliest which my inquiries have succeeded in obtaining, is 26th Nov. 1767, of the latest 22d June, 1808; the series as far as it extends being put into my hands as a perfect one; and in this series no statute to that effect, or on that subject, is to be found. The time at which it passed must therefore have been some time between some part of the year 1756 and the 26th November 1767, as above.

Thus often has this same code passed under review.

To what cause, then, is the country indebted for this continually open exhibition?—an enormous and multifarious mass of perpetually violated regulations, together with the oath by which obedience is promised to them, all left standing,—standing together for so many successive ages,—impregnating the whole population of this seat and source of Church of England religion, and from thence that of the whole country, with a perpetually inflowing stream of perjury?—Is it through inadvertence?—No:—but because in regularly Reverend and Right Reverend, not to speak of Honourable and Noble, eyes, if *perjury* be a bad sin, *innovation* is a still worse:—*innovation*, in which is included the removal of evil, in every shape in which it exists at present; *innovation*, in the exclusion of which is included the perpetuation of abuse, in every shape in which, at the expence of *the subject many*, profit is derived from it by *the ruling few*:—an exclusion, in which may be seen a fundamental—and not the less so for being so carefully locked up in the character of a secret —article, in the only "*Alliance*" ever spoken of that was not purely imaginary, "*between Church and State.*"

Thus far as to the additions made to the *subject-matter* of these oaths: now as to the additions made to the list of the *oaths themselves.*—While all existing oaths continued to be thus dealt with, fresh batches of the same species of pyecrust have continued to be issued out from the same sacred oven. May 1st, 1800, a new system of *examination* instituted, (examination for *degrees*): and the efficiency declared to be rested upon the strength of this perpetually broken reed. "*Tit.* ix. *Sect.* ii. *De Examinandis Graduum Candidatis*: § 1. *De Examinatoribus designandis et* Juramento onerandis *per Seniorem Procuratorem.*"

Some time in the year 1807, as may be inferred from the context (for there appears no date to it)—comes another Statute with the same title, repealing, but immediately in part re-enacting that so lately preceding one: innovating in this mode for the first time, and then no otherwise than upon a recent innovation: the first statute as far as appears, by which, since the days of *Laud*, so much as a single atom of the once consecrated mass was ever done away. By the same Reverend hands, the same *load* is now carefully reimposed on the same Reverend shoulders. With what degree of pressure and effect would any man be curious enough to calculate?—the *data* lie before him as above.

Moreover, though without any such idea stated as that of *load* or *burthen*, oaths have all along been sprinkled in on other occasions, and in other places, in and by the series of Statutes, 13 or 14 in number, passed in the interval between 1756 and 1813.

Thus much for *revisions* and *enactments*. Now as to *representations* and *remonstrances*.

In a book published by a Reverend Divine (*Vicesimus Knox*) then late a fellow of one of the Colleges in this same seat of piety and perjury—a book of which an edition published so long ago as the year 1789 was *the tenth*, —a book which accordingly has had a greater currency (and thus under the very eyes of the Reverend rulers in question) than perhaps ever fell to the lot of any book in which, in this or any other country, the subject of education has been touched upon—is inserted a Letter to the then *Chancellor, Lord North*, proposing a plan of reform, in which the species of perjury here in question forms the subject of the first article.

In holding up to view the universality, the constancy, the notoriety of this sin, together with the perfect consciousness of it in the minds of the Reverend persons whose lives were passed in the commission of it, are employed in different parts of this his work, directly or indirectly, no fewer than 54 out of its 727 pages.

In the representations thus made by Mr. Knox, are included others of the same tendency, which at different periods had been made by three other writers: viz. in 1721, by *Mr. Amhurst* under the title of *Terræ Filius*, in an anonymous periodical publication, reprinted in 2 vols. 12mo. in 1726: in 1725, by the Rev. *Dr. Newton*, Principal of Hart Hall, afterwards Hertford College, Oxford, in a tract intituled *University Education*, 8vo. pp. 209; and, in a year not specified, by R. Davies, M.D. of Queen's College, Cambridge, in a Letter to the Rev. Dr. Stephen Hales, the natural philosopher.

That remonstrance, though from a consecrated hand, having been productive of no other fruit than that of exposing the Reverend persons in question to a sort of censure, which being rather a passport than an obstruction to preferment, is of course to such persons a source rather of satisfaction than of uneasiness, the present attempt by a *lay* hand can not, howsoever *fruitless*, be charged with being *needless*.

III. *The principle of infallibility adhered to and acted upon to the last.*

In pages from 49 to 54, *infallibility* is mentioned as being among the attributes bestowed upon herself by the

English *Holy Mother Church*, and accordingly acknowledged, and worshipped, and shared in, by the academic part of her metaphorical progeny. To the eye which, either in the Memorials of the Puritan *Neale*, or in those of the orthodox and highly favoured *Strype*, can endure to look into it, the whole history of the Spiritual branch of the reign of *Elizabeth* is one continued body of evidence, concurring in the demonstration of this truth. Infallibility was the attribute of this church, under the governance of those princes of this church, whose thrones were subordinate to the throne of the Virgin Queen. These holy men were themselves *the Church:* and the royal mistress of their lives and fortunes—who could have expelled any of them for schism, or burnt any of them for heresy—being herself *the Church*, yea and more than the Church—was not only herself infallible, but the cause that infallibility was in *them*.

Of the assumption of this attribute follows one proof out of a thousand: if, in such a matter, *words* are less conclusively probative than *deeds*,—yet, in such a matter, neither are *words* without their value.

Anno 1584, "notwithstanding the charge of late given by Your Highness," (says *Archbishop Whitgift*, in a letter to the Queen, dated the 24th of March in that year) "notwithstanding the charge of late given by *Your Highness* to the lower House of Parliament, for dealing in the canon of the Church; albeit also, according to Your Majesty's good liking, *we* have sent down Order....yet have *they* passed a Bill in that House touching that matter;....*they* have also passed a Bill....contrary to the old canons continually observed among *us*, and containing matter which tendeth to the *slander of this* Church, as having hitherto *maintained an error* *."

To impute to this assemblage of constantly-corrupted and despot-ridden Churchmen—corrupted by hope of preferment, corrupted by dread of arbitrary and perpetually-impending deprivation, with ruin and either banishment or death at the end of it,—to such a set of men,

* *Strype's* Life of *Whitgift*, p. 198, in *Neale* § 457.

at a time too when Reason had but just begun to recover the use of her limbs,—the fact of having maintained an error—so much as one single error—this *a slander?* a slander, when coming from the mouth of Parliament! *This* Church! what Church?—The very Church which, after having so lately revolted from her antient Mother *the Church of Rome*, was,—at that very time, and in relation to these very points—in a state of separation from perhaps all her sister Churches;—from all other Protestant Churches;—and, at this very time, herself in a state of continual, and not as yet compleated, change.

In the very facility of making this change, by the same most reverend person is an argument found, for the putting an end for ever to all pretensions so unsuitable to the *limited*, and continually, so it were quietly, *reducible*, authority of an English Parliament.

"If it pass by Parliament," says he, "it cannot hereafter but in Parliament be altered....whereas, if it is but as a canon from *us*, by Your Majesty's authority, it may be observed or *altered* at pleasure."

In this document we have one out of a multitude, in which taken together it may be seen, how, of this Virgin Queen and *her little black husband* (so she was pleased to stile this her favourite Archbishop*) it was the acknowledged purpose, as well as practice, to persevere in a state of continual change, secure of being as continually infallible.

In theory such a horror of change,—and at the same time in intention as well as in practice so constant a state of change? all this self-contradiction how is it to be reconciled?—The change was to go on, till, under the name of *Puritans*, all those who, in matters of religion refused to change their belief, as well as practice, at the word of command as often as issued,—and whose real crime was the preferring a government *by* Parliament to a government *without* Parliament,—were extirpated: after which, unless for some equally good reason, there was to be no change. And such exactly was the result.

* *Cotton's* Life of *Hooker*, prefixed to his *Ecclesiastical Polity*, p. 23.

As the laws of the Medes and Persians, so the laws called the *Thirty-nine Articles*, (cut down as they were from a greater number) remained unchanged. But above the one code, as above the other, sat a despot, who, with his sub-despots, kept the rule of action—the inforced and efficient rule of action—viz. the will of those same despots—in a state of continual change.

So much for *infallibility*, and the *horror of innovation*: —the horror of innovation, which, being interpreted, is—the holy love of abuse, accompanied with the determination, by the blessing of Providence, to give every practicable increase to it.

IV. *Habitual perjury of the University Magistracy—further proof of its wilfulness.*

WHILE this last sheet is at the press, in comes the *Oxford University Calendar* for 1813, of I know not what series of Numbers the first that ever happened to meet my eye; and in it I read (p. 8.) the following passage:

"For the better government of the University, there is also an HEBDOMADAL MEETING OF THE HEADS OF HOUSES, who meet *every Monday*, and at other times when convened by the Vice-Chancellor. This meeting consists of the Vice-Chancellor, Heads of Houses and Proctors, who are empowered to deliberate upon all matters relating to the preservation of the privileges and liberties of the University, and *to inquire into, and consult respecting, the due observance of Statutes and Customs*."

In the seven preceding pages may be seen moreover a more detailed explanation of those arrangements in the constitutional branch of the law, whereby the principle of *infallibility* on the part of the legislature has been so systematically acted upon, and, in pursuance of it, the property of *immutability* given to the body of the laws, and with it that of *incorrigibility* to the defects with which they swarm, and the vices which they generate.

THE END.

CORRIGENDA.

Page.	Line.	
9	20	For *form* put *force.*
10	35	For *substitute* put *substantive.*
17	28	For *practices* put *operations.*
19	3	For *sure* put *surely.*
43	7	After *opponents:* dele *and*
55	31	For *section* put *sections.*
56	10	For *on* put *in.*
62	38	For *was* put *viz.*
84	10	Dele *in the production of the effect.*

Printed by R. & A. Taylor, Shoe Lane.

Lately published by the same Author,

A TABLE OF THE SPRINGS OF ACTION: shewing the several Species of Pleasures and Pains, of which Man's Nature is susceptible: together with the several Species of Interests, Desires, and Motives, respectively corresponding to them; and the several Sets of Appellatives Neutral, Eulogistic, and Dyslogistic, by which each Species of Motive is wont to be designated. To which are added EXPLANATORY NOTES AND OBSERVATIONS, indicative of the applications of which the matter of this Table is susceptible, in the character of a Basis or Foundation, of and for the Art and Science of Morals, otherwise termed Ethics,—whether Private, or Public *alias* Politics—(including Legislation)—Theoretical, or Practical *alias* Deontology—Exegetical *alias* Expository, (which coincides mostly with Theoretical,) or Censorial, which coincides mostly with Deontology: also of and for Psychology, in so far as concerns Ethics, and History (including Biography) in so far as considered in an Ethical point of view. Price 2*s*.

PLAN OF PARLIAMENTARY REFORM, in the Form of a CATECHISM, with Reasons for each Article; with an Introduction, shewing the Necessity of Radical and the Inadequacy of Moderate Reform. Price 8*s*.

Printed in Dunstable, United Kingdom

91221345R00060